THIS BOOK IS NOT TO BE
TAKEN FROM THE LIBRARY
AT ANY TIME.

D1713159

A Chaucer Gazetteer

FRANCIS P. MAGOUN, JR

A Chaucer Gazetteer

THE UNIVERSITY OF CHICAGO PRESS

The University of Chicago Press, Chicago 37
The University of Toronto Press, Toronto 5, Canada

Composition by
Almqvist & Wiksells Boktryckeri AB
Uppsala, Sweden, 1961

Printed and published 1961 by
The University of Chicago Press
Chicago, Illinois, U.S.A.

To HELGE KÖKERITZ
in Longstanding Friendship

PREFACE

THE PRESENT BOOK is a listing and discussion of all geographical names and names (uncapitalized) of geographical origin or with geographical connections, such as *brazile*, *chalon*, used by Geoffrey Chaucer. It is essentially a conflation of three earlier papers with a few minor additions, adjustments and corrections: 'Chaucer's Ancient and Biblical World', *Mediaeval Studies* XV (1953), 107–36, 'Chaucer's Great Britain', *ibid.*, XVI (1954), 131–56, and 'Chaucer's Mediaeval World outside of Great Britain', *ibid.*, XVII (1955), 117–42. For permission to use this material I am grateful to the publishers of *Mediaeval Studies*, the Pontifical Institute of Mediaeval Studies, Toronto, Ontario, Canada.

Beside listing the names and citing their places of occurrence I have tried to indicate how and in what specific connection these names are used and have included references to passages where they are implied, where *Rome* may be referred to as a *cité* or *toun* and the like, in order to give as complete a picture as possible of Chaucer's notions about a place. This same general scheme I first followed in 'Geographical and Ethnic Names in the *Nibelungenlied*', *Mediaeval Studies* VII (1945), 85–138. I have made no attempt to furnish etymologies for Classical or Biblical names since these are in so many cases obscure and in almost any event would have little meaning to most readers of Chaucer including the present writer, but etymologies are given for all or almost all other names including British and Continental place-names, many of which have an interesting background.

Any consideration of these names *en masse* and for themselves can give the reader a very fair idea of the range of Chaucer's geographical knowledge, even though many must have been merely names to him. For a fuller discussion of this aspect of the subject the reader is referred to the forewords to the original three papers.

Certain names, set in square brackets to indicate that they are not used by Chaucer, are listed because, though the place is not mentioned, its existence is implicit and matters concerning it can ony be discussed in an orderly fashion under the name itself set up as a head-word, as in the case of [*Knaresborough*], [*Westminster*, *City of*,] and others.

Finally I would express my gratitude to Mr Ojars Kratins of the Harvard Graduate School of Arts and Sciences for carrying out the task of conflating the original papers.

F. P. M., Jr

Cambridge, Massachusetts, 1960

ABBREVIATIONS

The key-words (and a few variants) are taken from Fred N. Robinson's *The Works of Geoffrey Chaucer* (2d ed.), as are the line numbers; title-abbreviations are those of the John S. P. Tatlock and A. G. Kennedy *Concordance to the Complete Works of Chaucer*, whose line-numbers in the case of the *Astrolabe* and *Boethius*, as well as the book and line numbers of books 2 and 3 of the *Hous of Fame* are given parenthetically after Robinson's number. References to the B group of the *Canterbury Tales*, broken up by Robinson into B¹ and B², are given as in Robinson: the break comes at B 1190 and in the continuous numbering B² lines are preceded by an asterisk, i.e., B *1191 ff. The independent numbering for B² follows this in parentheses and without special designation. *Y* is everywhere alphabeted in with *i*.

Berks	Berkshire
B & D	William Frank Bryan and Germaine Dempster *et al.*, edd., *Sources and Analogues of Chaucer's Canterbury Tales* (Chicago University Press, 1941)
Bowden	Muriel Bowden, *A Commentary on the General Prologue to the Canterbury Tales* (New York: Macmillan, 1949)
C	Cambridgeshire
Cook	Albert Stanborough Cook, "The Historical Background of Chaucer's Knight", *Transactions of the Connecticut Academy of Arts and Sciences*, XX (1916), 161–240
Cowley	J. M. C(owley), "Chaucer's Bob-Up-and-Down", *The Athenaeum, Journal of Literature, Science and the Fine Arts*, July to December 1868, p. 886 (26 December 1868); reprinted in Furnivall 32–34, Littlehales 36–38

C & S–W   Samuel Hazzard Cross and Olgerd P. Sherbowitz-
            Wetzor, transl., *The Russian Primary Chronicle*:
            Laurentian Text (Cambridge, Mass.: Mediaeval
            Academy of America, 1953)
D   Devonshire
Darby   Harry Clifford Darby, ed., *An Historical Geography
            of England before A.D. 1800* (Cambridge, 1936)
DEPN   Eilert Ekwall, *The Concise Dictionary of English
            Place-Names* (3d ed., Oxford, 1947)
DNB   *The Dictionary of National Biography*, original
            issue Oxford 1885–90, reprinted 1921–22. Cited
            by volume and page
Du Cange   Sieur [Dominus] Du Cange (né Charles Du Fresne),
            Glossarium Mediae et Infimae Latinitatis, etc., 7
            vols (Paris, 1840–50)
EB   *Encyclopaedia Britannica*, 14th ed. (London–New
            York, 1929)
EI   *Enciclopedia Italiana di scienze, letteres ed arte*
            (Rome 1929–37)
E Isl   *Encyclopaedia of Islam* (Leyden, 1913–38)
ERN   Eilert Ekwall, *English River-Names* (Oxford,
            1928)
Ess   Essex
EUI   *Enciclopedia Universal Ilustrada* (Barcelona, 1912–
            33), with continuing supplements
Förster   *Themse* Max Förster, "Der Flussname Themse
            und seine Sippe", *Sitzungsberichte der bayerischen
            Akademie der Wissenschaften*, phil.-histor. Abtei-
            lung, 1941, I
Fr   French
Furnivall   Frederick J. Furnivall, *Temporary Preface to the
            Six-Text Edition of Chaucer's Canterbury Tales*,
            Part I (Chaucer Society Publ., 2 d Ser. 3, London,
            1868)
G & I   Boris D. Grekov and A. Iakoubovski, François
            Thuret transl., *La Horde d'or: la domination tatare
            au XIIIe et au XIVe siècle de la Mer Jaune à la*

	Mer Noire (Paris, 1939); there is a later edition of the Russian original
Gl	Gloucestershire
Gröhler	Hermann Gröhler, *Über Ursprung und Bedeutung der französischen Ortsnamen*, 2 vols (Heidelberg, 1913, 1933)
Herts	Hertfordshire
Holder	Alfred Holder, *Alt-Celtischer Sprachschatz*, 3 vols, including addenda to Vol. I (Leipzig, 1896–1913)
Jerrold	Walter C. Jerrold, *Highways and Byways in Kent* (London, 1907)
K	Kent
Lawrence	William Witherle Lawrence, *Chaucer and the Canterbury Tales* (New York: Columbia University Press, 1950)
Littlehales	Henry Littlehales, *Some Notes on the Road from London to Canterbury in the Middle Ages* (Chaucer Society Publ., 2d Ser. 30, London, 1898)
Longnon	Auguste Longnon, *Les Noms de lieu de la France*, etc. (Paris, 1920)
Lowes	John Livingston Lowes, "The Dry Sea and the Carrenare", *Modern Philology*, III (1905–06), 1–46
Manly	John Matthews Manly, *Canterbury Tales by Geoffrey Chaucer*, corrected printing (New York, 1928)
Matthias	Walther Matthias, *Die geographische Nomenclatur Italiens im altdeutschen Schrifttum* (Leipzig, 1912)
MED	*Middle English Dictionary* (Ann Arbor, Michigan: University of Michigan Press, 1952 ff.)
MHG	Middle High German
M–L	Wilhelm Meyer-Lübke, *Romanisches etymologisches Wörterbuch*, 3d edition (Heidelberg, 1935)
MLG	Middle Low German
MR	John M. Manly and Edith Rickert, *The Text of the Canterbury Tales Studied on the Basis of All Known Manuscripts*, 8 vols (Chicago, 1940). Cited by volume and page

MS	*Mediaeval Studies* (Toronto, Ontario: The Pontifical Institute of Mediaeval Studies, 1938 ff.)
Muirhead	*England* L. Russel Muirhead, ed., *England* ("The Blue Guides"), 5th edition (London, 1950)
Muirhead	*London* Findlay Muirhead, *London and its Environs*, 3d ed. (London, 1927)
Mx	Middlesex
NED	*A New* (alias *Oxford*) *English Dictionary*, etc. (Oxford, 1888–1928). Cited by words
Nf	Norfolk
NGF	Joseph Mansion, "Die voornaamste Bestanddeelen der vlaamsche Plaatsnaamen", *Nomina geographica Flandrica, Studiën*, Vol. III (Brussels, 1935)
Nissen	Heinrich Nissen, *Italienische Landeskunde*, 2 vols in 3 pts (Berlin, 1883–1909)
O	Oxfordshire
OE	Old English
OFr	Old French
OGN	Joseph Mansion, *Oud-Gentsche Naamkunde* ('s-Gravenhagen, 1924)
Olivieri	Dante Olivieri, *Dizionario di Toponomastica Lombarda* (Milan, 1931)
Owen	Charles A. Owen, Jr., "The Plan of the Canterbury Pilgrimage", *Publications of the Modern Language Ass'n of America*, LXVI (1951), 820–26.
PN	English Place-Name Society, publications (Cambridge, 1925 ff.), with volume number, followed by the appropriate county abbreviation
Pratt	Robert A. Pratt, "The Order of the Canterbury Tales", *Publications of the Modern Language Ass'n of America*, LXVI (1951), 1141–67
Reallexikon	Johannes Hoops *et al.*, edd., *Reallexikon der germanischen Altertumskunde*, 4 vols (Strassburg-im-Elsass, 1911–18)
Repetti	Emanuele Repetti, *Dizionario geographico-fisico-storico della Toscana*, 6 vols (Florence, 1833–46)
Robinson	Fred Norris Robinson, ed., *The Complete Works of*

	Geoffrey Chaucer, 2d revised ed. (Boston: Hough-ton Mifflin, 1957)
Sa	Shropshire
Sf	Suffolk
Skeat	Walter W. Skeat, ed., *The Complete Works of Geoffrey Chaucer*, 7 vols (Oxford, 1894–97). Cited by volume and page
Skeat *PPl*	*idem.*, ed., *The Vision of William concerning Piers the Plowman ... together with Richard the Redeless*, 2 vols (Oxford, 1886). Cited by volume and page
So	Somersetshire
Sr	Surrey
Tatlock	John Strong Perry Tatlock, "The Duration of the Canterbury Pilgrimage", *Publications of the Modern Language Ass'n of America*, XXI (1906), 478–85
Tatlock *FT*	*idem.*, *The Scene of the Franklin's Tale Visited* (London: Chaucer Society, 2d Ser., No. 51, 1914)
W & P	Alois Walde and Josef Pokorny, *Vergleichendes Wörterbuch der indogermanischen Sprachen*, 3 vols (Berlin, 1930–32)
YER	Yorkshire, East Riding
YNR	Yorkshire, North Riding
YWR	Yorkshire, West Riding

A

Achademycis, see **At(t)henes.**

Achaleous, the river Achelous [Lat. *Acheloüs*], mod. Aspropotamos, rising in Mt Pindus (mod. Mezzara) and emptying into the Ionian Sea, is in *Bo* 4, m. 7, l. 47 (1605–10) a *flod*, mentioned in connection with the story of Hercules's successful struggle against the river-god of the same name (cp. also *CT* B *3296 [2106]).

Chaucer's form would seem, if not accidental, to be based on a Gk type gen. vs Boethius' *Achelous amnis.*

Achemenye [Lat. *Achaemenia*], the Persian (Achaemenian) Empire of the Achaemenides (OPers. *Hakhamanishiya*), a dynasty at its height in the time of Cyrus and Darius and later kings, would in *Bo* 5, m. 1, l. 3 (1640–45) seem to refer specifically to the province of Parthia (mod. Khorasan), being mentioned as a *contré* whose warriors in true or feigned flight would turn on their foes and shoot at them ("Parthian shot") (ll. 4–6). It is also the realm in whose rocky highlands (*cragges of the roche*, ll. 2–3; Boethius' *rupis Achaemenidae*) are wrongly said to rise from a single source (*o welle*, l. 2) the Euphrates and the Tigris (see *Eufrates*, *Tigris*, below).

Chaucer's form is French.

Aegean Sea, the Aegean [Lat. *[Mare] Aegeum*], extending eastward from Greece to Asia Minor, is referred to as *see* in *HF* 417, *LGW* 1462, 1470, 1495, 1510, 2178, 2196, 2405, 2419; in 2163 it is described as *wilde.*

Afrike [Auffrike] [Lat. *Africa*], Africa:

A. Reflecting the original Carthaginian application of the ethnic name *Afer*, plur. *Afri*, to the peoples of the area of Carthage (*Cartage*, below) and/or Libya (*Libie*, below), hence virtually synonymous with Carthage or Libya. In *HF* 431 *Auffrikes regioun* is Libya, in l. 432 it is more closely identified with Dido's *faire toun* (of Carthage). In *Bo* 2, pr. 6, l. 78 (500–05) *men of Affryke* are Carthaginians taken prisoners by Marcus Atilius Regulus in the course of the First Punic War. In *PF* 37 Scipio Africanus (Chaucer's *Affrican*, etc.) comes to *Affrike* to meet the Numidian prince Massinissa (see under *Cartage*) on which occasion (*CT* B *4314 [3124]) Scipio has a vision portending the fall of Carthage.

B. By extension this name comes to apply to the whole continent and is thus used in *HF* 1339 (3, 249).

Chaucer's form is French, mod. *Afrique*.

Albyon, Albion, literary-poetical designation of Britain, here specifically England, is mentioned in *Purse* 22 as the realm of a conqueror who "*by lyne and free eleccion*" (*Purse* 23) won the country in question. The words defining this ruler's position (*conqueror*) and his claim (by lineage and free election) can only refer to Henry IV (*regn.* 1399–1413) who instituted for himself or for whom was instituted a sort of threefold hold or claim on popular allegiance. See "Henry IV", *DNB* IX, 487, col. 1 at top.

On the name "Albion" being used for all Britain or even just for England vs its later restricted application to Scotland, see Eilert Ekwall, *Antiquity*, IV (1930), 149–50. Celt.*Albion means "white country" (cognate with Lat. *albus*), presumably from the white cliffs of the coast.

Alcathoe, Alcathoe [Lat. *Alcathoe, -es*, f.], citadel of ancient Megara on the Saronic Gulf, now the Gulf of Aegina, S of Athens, and chief town of ancient Megaris. It is mentioned with reference to the *sege* by Minos, legendary king of Crete (*LGW* 1909), and in *LGW* 1902, 1923; it is a *cité* (*LGW* 1904, 1916) with strong *walles* (1903). *Other tounes moo* mentioned with Alcathoe in *LGW* 1923 refer to other cities in Greece in general.

Chaucer's form is Latin; the name is based on the personal name *Alcathoüs*, son of Pelops, legendary founder of Megara.

Alexandryn, adj. [*land A.*, var. *land of A.*], of or pertaining to Alexandria (*Alisaundre*, below), Alexandrine; *land (of) A.* means the region centering on Alexandria and by extension probably includes the East or Near East in general as a source of things exotic; it is the part of the world whence the head-gardener Mirth imported trees for the garden of the Rose (*RR* 602). The contemporary city is here to be assumed.

The received text (ed. Ernest Langlois) of the *Roman de la Rose* 592 reads *la terre as Sarradins* (var. *Sarrasins*) "Saracen country" but several manuscripts have *terre Alixandrin(s)*, and so obviously Chaucer's copy of the OFr text.

Algezir [var. MR V, 6], Algeciras (prov. Cadiz), Spain, seaport 6 m. W of *Jubaltare*, is mentioned in *CT* A 57 as a place at the siege of which (1344? 1369?) the Knight had been; see Cook 217–28, Robinson 652, col. 1.

In antiquity *Portus Albus*, also *Julia Joza, Julia Transducta*, the present name is adapted from Arab. *al-Djazira (al-Qadra)* "(Green) Island", apparently from the verdure of the region, reflected still in *Isla Verde* just offshore (*E Isl* I, 277). For various rather distorted OFr forms, see Cook 217; Chaucer's form is a shortening of the Spanish name, presumably by way of French.

Alisaundre, Alexandria, Arab. *al- Iskenderieh* [Lat. *Alexandrea, -ia*], Egypt. Located at the mouth of the Nile delta, Alexandria (founded B.C. 332), the most important of several—according to the *Historia de Preliis Alexandri Magni* § 131, twelve—cities established by Alexander the Great, ranked only second to Rome for many centuries and for some thousand years was the capital of Egypt. In the Middle Ages it was a great emporium of trade with the East; it lost much of its importance with the discovery in 1498 of the route to the East via the Cape of Good Hope.

A. With reference to its greatness in antiquity it is mentioned in *CT* G 975 in association with the ancient cities of *Nyneve(e)*, *Rome*, and *Troie*.

B. In *CT* A 51 and B*3582 (2392) it is mentioned in connection with its temporary conquest by Peter I, king of Cyprus, in 1365 (Manly 499–500; Robinson 652, col. 1, 745, n. 2391; Bowden 55–56); in *BD* 1025 it is one of a number of places remote from France or England to which a difficult lady might dispatch her courtly lover.

Chaucer's form is based on the OFr form of the name *Alixandre* (mod. Fr *Alexandrie*) with the characteristic Norman *au*.

Amazones [Lat. *Amazon, -es*, f.] Amazons, warlike women, who according to ancient tradition lived on the banks of the Thormodon, mod. Turk. *Terme cayı*, are mentioned in *CT* A 880 in connection with their defeat by the Athenians and the marriage of their queen Hippolyta to Theseus, king of Athens. Their kingdom is *Femenie*, equated with *Scithia*.

[Ambracian Gulf], [Lat. *Sinus Ambracius*], mod. Gulf of Arta at the mouth of the Arta (ancient *Arachthus*) on the NW coast of Greece, is referred to as a *see* in *LGW* 634 in connection with the Battle of Actium (mod. Punta), site of the Emperor Octavian's naval victory over Mark Antony B.C. 31.

Apennyn [var. MR VI, 247], the Apennine range or the Apennines, central mountain system of Italy, is described in *CT* E 45 as *hilles hye*, in E 46 said to form the western boundary of *Lumbardye*.

The name in this form (singular) looks back to Roman (Ligurian?) *Apenninus* (*Mons*), used by Petrarch and modernized by Chaucer; the modern forms are usually plural: Ital. *Appennini* (but *Appennino* sg. for the range as a whole), Fr. *Apennins*, English *Apennines*.

Arabik, adj.-sb. Arabic, the language of the mediaeval Arabian scientists, is mentioned in *Astr.Prol.* 37 (5–11).

Chaucer's form may either reflect Lat. *arabicus* or OFr *arabique*.

Arab(y)e [Lat. *Arabia*], Arabia, the Arabian peninsula, is mentioned in *BD* 982 to define the legendary phoenix bird, sometimes associated with Arabia Felix. In *CT* F 110 *Arabe* (var. *Arabye*) is the realm of an unnamed thirteenth-century ruler said also to rule *Inde* (see below).

Chaucer's form is French, mod. *Arabie*. The form *Arabe* of *CT* F 110 is either a scribal error or, more likely, due to confusion with the French form of the ethnic name *Arabe* 'an Arab.'

Arabyen, adj. subst., an Arabian, Arab, inhabitant of the Arabian peninsula:

A. Used in *CT* B *3529 (2339) in a catalog of peoples who in the third century A.D. dared not oppose Queen Zenobia of Palmyra (see *Palymerie*, below).

B. In *Astr*. *Pr*. 36 (5–11) reference is to Arab scholars of the eighth century A.D.; in *Astr*. Pt. I, § 10, l. 8 (45–50) *arabiens* is a plur. adj.

Arabyen, mod. Fr. *arabien* as if from Lat. *Arabianus, is based on the regional name Arabia (see *Arabye*, above).

Aragon, Aragon [Span. Aragón], region and ancient kingdom comprising the present-day Spanish provinces of Huesca, Zaragoza, Teruel, lies just W of *Cataloigne* with which it formed in Chaucer's day a joint kingdom. Along with *Cataloigne* it is mentioned in *HF* 1248 (3, 158) (:*clarion*) as a land notable for its clarion- or trumpet-players. On the festive and ceremonial role of the trumpet in this region in the thirteenth, hence presumably in Chaucer's fourteenth century, see Higini Anglès, *La Musica a Catalunya fino al segle XIII* (Barcelona, 1953), a reference for which I am most grateful to Dr Walter Muir Whitehill. Chaucer could have learned of the practice of this art in Catalonia and Aragon through many channels.

The regional name is based on the river-name Aragón; Chaucer's form shows the Spanish stress on the ultima.

Arcadye [Lat. *Arcadia*], Arcadia, central mountainous province of the Peloponnesus, is mentioned quite incidentally in *Bo* 3, m. 3, ll. 18–19 (1315–20) (*Mercurie ... the bridd of Arcadye*) with reference to the legendary birth-place of the god Mercurius Cyllenius on Mt Cyllene (see *Cilenios*, below) in NE

Arcadia; the god is spoken of as a bird because of being traditionally figured with wings (cp. *the winged god Mercurie*, *CT*
A 1385).

Chaucer's form is French, mod. *Arcadie*.

Ardea [Lat. *Ardea*], Ardea, a town 23 m. S of Rome in Latium, capital of Turnus and the tribe of the Rutuli, also said
to have been burned by Aeneas; from the ashes of the town the
heron (*ardea*) was said to have been engendered. In *LGW* 1694
Ardea is mentioned in connection with a siege by the Romans
in the reign of Lucius Tarquinius Superbus (*regn.* 534–10 B.C.).
In *LGW* 1730 it is a *place*, its *walles* are mentioned in 1726; the
sege is referred to in 1696, 1725, 1758.

Chaucer's form is Latin.

Arge, Argon [Lat. *Argos* sg., more frequently *Argi* plur.],
chief city and district of the peninsula of Argolis in the NE
Peloponnesus, mod. Morea. It is mentioned together with
Calidoigne (see below) as the realm of Diomedes of the Homeric
Age in *TC* 5, 805, 934, and as *Argon that cité*, the city proper,
in *LGW* 2682, answering to Ovid's *Heroides* 14, 34: *quies alta
per Argos erat*, where it is probably poetical for all Greece.

Chaucer's *Arge* looks back to OFr *Arge(s)* vs mod. *Argos*;
Chaucer's *Argon* represents somehow a Gk acc. of *Argos*.

Argeyes, Argives, people of Argos (see *Arge*, above), are
mentioned in *TC* 5, 1501, where they are said to be ruled by
Tydeus, historically the father—in Chaucer wrongly the grandfather—of Diomedes. See also *Argyves*, below.

Argon, see *Arge*, above.

Argyves [Lat. *Argivus*], Argives, people of Argos, poetical for Greeks in general, is mentioned in *TC* 5, 1509. A sing. form *Argyve*, as if an "Argive woman", occurs in *TC* 4, 762, as Chaucer's invented name of Criseyde's mother, in turn by error or curious confusion presumably somehow based on the personal name *Argia*.

Chaucer's form derives from OFr *Argive*, pl.-*es*. Cp. *Argeyes*.

Armorik(e) [var. MR VI, 577, 612; VII, 510], Armorica (Old Breton *Armorik*, later Breton *Arvorek*, -*ik*), formally answers to Gallo-Lat. *Aremoricae*, referring to some of the coastal region of latter-day Brittany and Normandy; in *CT* F 729 it is equated with *Britaigne* II as the scene of the main part of the Franklin's Tale. In *CT* B² *3578 (2388) it is the homeland of Genylon-Oliver, i.e., a Ganelon-type Oliver or completely disloyal friend; see Robinson 749, col. 1.

The name is based on Gaulish *ar-* "on, upon" and *mor-* "sea" with reference to the lay of the land; on this name, see further Holder I, 202–03; Max Förster, Herrig's *Archiv*, CXLVI (1923), 134. With similar implications are Irish *Letha* and Welsh *Llydaw*, based on the stem *līt-* in Lat. *lītus* "shore", both being names for Britanny and with similar implications; cp. *Lettow*. Chaucer's form is adapted from Fr. *Armorique* in turn looking back to Med. Lat. *Armorica* (sing.).

Arras, Arras on the Scarpe (dép. Pas-de-Calais) in northern France and chief city of the county of *Artoys*, is referred to in *RR* 1234 (*Roman de la Rose* 1212) in praising a suckeny or smock worn by Franchise, said to be the fairest *in all Arras*; in the French text the *sorquenie* "suckeny" is said to be the richest from anywhere to Arras (*n'ot si riche jusqu'a Arraz*). Arras was early known for its woollen manufacture and production of tapestries (see *NED s.v.* "arras"). The original name of the place was *Nemetocen(n)a*; Holder II, 711.

The name looks back o the Gallo-Lat. tribal name *Atrebates* "possessors, residents" (Holder I, 267–71), later contracted to *Atradis, Atrasi(civitas)*, OE *Aðerats* (*MS* II, 248), whence the modern form; see further Gröhler I, 89, Longnon No. 413.

Artoys, Artois, ancient countship of *Fraunce*, bounded on the N by *Flaundres*, on the S by *Pycardie*, and corresponding in the main to the modern department of Pas-de-Calais, is mentioned in *CT* A 86 along with *Flaundres* and *Pycardie* as the scene of the Squire's military activities. His *chyvachie* (A 85) is possibly with reference to the 1369 campaign of Edward III or to the so-called crusade (1383) of Henry le Despenser, bishop of Norwich; see Robinson 754, Squire, headnote. The name is today most familiar in London and elsewhere in 'Stella Artois', the name of a popular imported light lager beer.

Like *Arras*, this regional name looks back to the tribal name *Atrebates*, specifically (*pagus*) *Atrebatensis*; Gröhler I, 89; Longnon No. 413. Cp. *Paris* for a similar substitution of a tribal name for a place-name.

Asye [Lat. *Asia*], Asia, originally probably a name for a town in ancient Lydia (*Lyde*, below) or for Lydia itself; as extended to include all Asia Minor it is a late Roman term.

A. It is used presumably in this earlier sense of Asia Minor in *CT* B *1678 (488) to identify an imaginary Christian settlement (*a greet cité*) with a Jewish quarter (see *Jewerye*, below) in an unnamed *contré* (B *1680 [490]).

B. In *HF* 1339 (3, 249) it refers to the whole continent of

Asia, mentioned in connection with Europe and Africa.

Chaucer's form is French (Mod. Fr. *Asie*).

At(t)henes, Athenys [Lat. *Athenae*], Athens, chief city of ancient Attica and of the modern kingdom of Greece. It is referred to mostly in the *Legend of Ariadne* and in the *Knight's Tale*, often in most general connections, sometimes defining a ruler (duke, governor, king, lord, prince): *HF* 388 (1, 388), 1228 (3, 138), *Anel* 46, *LGW head* (between 1885–86), 1897, 1922, 1944, 2122, *end* (between 2227–28), 2128, 2361, 2406, 2442, *CT* A 861, 873, 880, 968, 973, 1023, 1194, 1391, 1395, 1406, 1413, 2098, 2483, 2701, 2964, 2971, F 1369. It is a *cité* in *LGW* 1899, 1904, *CT* A 1066 (*noble*), 1287, 2188, 2191, 2567 (*large*), 2574, 2701, 2902; a *place* in *LGW* 1915; a *toun* in *Bo* 5, m. 4, l. 2 (1805–10); *LGW* 1942, *CT* A 894, 973, 1628, 2189, 2738, 2829. Athenians are referred to as *hem of Athenes* in *Bo* 1, pr. 5, l. 21 (200–05), and *LGW* 1925, 1940. Though not directly mentioned, the port town of Piraeus, some five miles from Athens, is assumed in *LGW* 2552 (*haven of Athenes*), 2361, 2509; in 2305–06 it is suggested that the main street (*maysterstrete*) leads from the city to the harbor, also in *CT* A 2902, 2904 (*strete*). *Athenes*, mentioned in *LGW* 1965–66, is some kind of slip for Crete.

Within the town is the Stoa or *Porch* of Zeno (*Bo* 5, m. 4 ll. 1, 2, 4 [1805–10]), defined as a *gate*, perhaps in the sense of a "passage way" rather than a "gate". Demophon's *palace large* is mentioned in *LGW* 2406, Theseus' palace in *CT* A 2199 (with a dais), 2494, 2513, 2525 (*riche*), 2527, with a *halle* or great hall in A 2521, the king's *chambre* (A 2525) and a *wyndowe* (A 2528). The latter is likewise referred to as a *court* in A 1414, 1430, 1497 (*roial*), 1504, with a gate (A 1415), and in A 1057 as a *castel*. Adjacent is Emelye's walled garden (A 1051, 1060 [*gardyn wal*], 1067, 1099, 1105), referred to as a *place* in A 1119. Overlooking the garden and built on to the garden wall is the main *tour* (A 1030, 1056, 1277), and constituting the main keep (*dongeon*, A 1057) of Theseus' castle was a *priso(u)n* high up (A 1023, 1058, 1085, 1095, 1107, 1109, 1185, 1206, 1229, 1236, 1237, 1335, 1451, 1468, 1562, 1592, 1735, 1792), in which was a *chambre* (A 1065, 1071) with a heavily barred window (A 1075–76). In the town is a temple of Isis (*HF* 1844–45 [3, 754–55]).

Leading out of the town is a highway (A 897: *the heighe wey*) and in the outskirts a temple of the goddess Clementia (A 928), also lodgings for visitors (*hostelryes*, A 2493). Farther out begin *feeld(es)* (A 1503, 1632), the open country of the Attic plain, and a mile or two out (A 1504) is a *grove* (A 1478, 1481, 1505, 1514, 1635, 2860, 2898) with a brook (A 1693) and a *launde* or clearing (A 1691, 1696). Likewise a mile or so NW of the ancient city out in the country on the banks of the Cephissus, flowing into the Saronic Gulf, is the Academy (Lat. *Academia*) founded by Plato *ca* B.C. 387 and presided over by him until his death B.C. 348. Its existence is implied in the phrase "*in the studies and scoles of Eleaticis* (see *Elea*, below) *and Achademycis in Grece*" (Lat. dat. pl.) (*Bo* 1, pr. 1, l. 74 [30–35]), an awkward rendering of Boethius' *in studiis et scholis Eleaticis et Academicis*.

The most conspicuous architectural monument of Theseus' Athens is a bowl-type stadium, presumably outside the town walls, and constructed by Theseus especially for the tournament between Palamon and Arcite. Referred to as a *theatre* (A 1885, 1901, 2091), a *place* (A 2585, 2678, 2690), and more often as *lystes* (A 1884, 2089, 2218, 2545, 2566, 2575, 2662), it is a circular stone structure (A 1889) with a moat (*walled of stoon and dyched al withoute*, A 1888), 1 mile in circumference, 60 paces high (*pas*, A 1890), and with rising tiers of seats (*degrees*, A 1890, 1891, 2579) banked to afford the spectator an unobstructed view (A 1892), also called *seetes* in A 2580. The number of rows of seats is not specified; the stadium is said to be *ful of degrees*, i.e., tiers of seats (A 1890). The full diameter must be thought of as some 560 yards, the height perhaps 150 feet, if one modestly reckons a "pace" as *ca* 2½ feet. Stadium builders tell me that the playing surface might be reckoned as some 1000 feet in diameter, corresponding to a king-size polo field, and that the edifice might have seated a couple of hundred thousand people. The Colosseum of ancient Rome seated about 45,000; the world's largest stadium in Rio de Janeiro seats 175,000 spectators. About a year was allowed for the construction of the Theseus Bowl (A 1850–51), in which many engineers, craftsmen and artists took part (A 1897–1901) and was done at great cost (A 2090). The Theseus Bowl was not only by all odds the world's biggest stadium but was handsome as well. At the east and west points of the circle were white marble *gates*, the main entries (A 1893–94, 1909; 2597); above the east entry was a chapel or shrine (*oratorie*, A 1904–05, 2585) dedicated to Venus; above the west entry one to Mars (A 1906–07, 2581); while on the north side in a *touret* springing from the outer wall is a third oratory dedicated to Diana (A 1909–12); these are referred to as *thise oratories thre* in A 1917 and are characterized by elaborate murals. Despite the term *temple* applied to them in A 1918 (cp. 2663), 2218, 2251–52 (with an altar) (of Venus); 1969, 1982, 2009, 2368, 2407, 2410, 2422, 2425–26 (with an altar) (of Mars); A 2051, 2281 (of Diana), these shrines should not be thought of as "temples" in the sense of Lat. *templum* but

rather as Lat. *aedis* which by *interpretatio christiana* is well
described by the word *oratorie*. From his experience as Clerk
of the King's Works (1389–90) Chaucer might have learned
much about elaborate construction of this sort though he had
certainly written up this material or an earlier equivalent much
earlier. On Boccacio's account of Teseo's theatre in the *Teseida*
see R. A. Pratt, *PMLA*, LXII (1947), 100 and notes; on Chaucer's adjustment of Boccacio's treatment of the oratories see
Pratt, *ibid.*, 617–18.

Chaucer's form of the name, whence mod. Athens, looks
back to OFr *Athenes* (Lat. *Athenas*).

[**Attica**], not directly mentioned, may be inferred in *contré* in
LGW 2053, 2057, 2176, 2472; *CT* A 869, 1213, and *land* in
LGW 2154, 2478, *CT* A 1725, also more indirectly by *home-
ward* (*LGW* 2162) and *contréward* (*LGW* 2176).

B

Babilan, this curious form, perhaps for *Babilon*, used for
"of Babylon the city" or "of the region of Babylonia", "Baby-
lonian", is applied in *CT* B 63 to Thisbe of ancient legend. The
adjective form may be based on the OFr type of the city-name
Babilon(n)e "Babylon", by-form of the more usual *Babiloigne*,
below.

Babiloigne [Lat. *Babylonia*], famous Euphrates city of Babylon, is mentioned in connection with more than one period of
its history.

A. In *CT* B *3339 (2149) it is the principal seat (*sovereign see*)
of the empire of Nebuchadrezzar II the Assyrian (*regn.* 605–

562 B.C.), famed for its wealth (*BD* 1060–61), referring either to the city or the province.

B. In *CT* B *3374 (2184), *3380 (2190), *3404 (2214), *3424 (2234) it is the kingdom or realm (*regne*) of Belshazzar or Balsharazur, son of Nebuchadrezzar and last king of Babylon.

C. In *CT* D 2082 it is the goal of conquest of Cyrus the Great, who entered the city in 539 B.C.

D. Most references occur in the "Legend of Thisbe" and refer to the legendary period of Queen Semiramis (Sammuramat) and of Pyramus and Thisbe (*LGW* 706 ff.). Here the outlying region of Babylonia, not mentioned by name, is referred to as a *lond* (*LGW* 716, *CT* B *3397 [2207]), as a (Near-) Eastern country (*lond estward*, *LGW* 718), and as a *contré* (*LGW* 721).

The city itself is a (*noble*) *toun* (*LGW* 707, 710), a *cité* (781). Semiramis, widow of King Ninus, had a moat built about the city (*let dychen al aboute*, 708) and high ramparts built of hard well-baked tiles (*walles ful hye of harde tiles wel ybake*, 708–09). The unnamed fathers of Pyramus and Thisbe are said to have their estates on an open space (*grene*, 712) in the city, separated only by a wall (*stonwall*, 713, *wall* 737, 750, 754, 756), evidently badly in want of repair, for it has a crack (*clyfte*, 740 ff.) of long standing which runs from the foundation to the top of the wall. A good deal is told about the outlying countryside. There is open country (*feldes*, 782, 787), a wood (*wode*, 806, 822; *forest*, 842) infested with lions (cp. *wilde lyonesse*, 805 ff.); King Ninus, legendary eponymous of Nineveh (see *Nynyvee* below), was buried out there (785). There was a cave in the vicinity (811), also a well or spring (*welle*, 788, 804, 808, 818). The sun is said to set beneath the sea (*se*, 792), though Babylon was some 500–600 miles east of the Mediterranean.

Chaucer's form looks back to OFr *Babiloigne*, in turn a normal development of Lat. *Babilonia*, properly the name of the region.

Babilonia [Lat.], whose genitive *Babilonie* is used in *LGW* 706 *head* to define Thisbe (*Tesbe*). See *Babiloigne*, above.

Baldeswelle [var. MR V, 58], Bawdeswell in northern Nf, is mentioned in *CT* A 620 as the town near which the bailiff or *Reve* Oswald lived: the village is 3 m. SW of Reepham-with-Kerdiston (Nf). Muirhead *England* 603; Manly 532; Bowden 254–55.

The name looks back to OE *Beald-heres wielle* "Beald-here's spring".

Barbarie, vaguely the ancient pagan world, throughout which is said (*CT* F 1452) to be famous Artemisia, wife of Mausolus, king or dynast of Caria (approx. the mod. Turkish prov. of Aydin and Denizli) (d. *ca* 353 B.C.) and on whose death Artemisia built a magnificent tomb, the first "mausoleum".

The name reflects an OFr adaptation of Lat. (*terra*) *barbaria* "foreign, barbarous country"; the name is not to be confused geographically with the later-day Barbary, Barbary Coast, and the like.

[biside] Bathe, [near, juxta] Bath (So) on the Avon, is always mentioned to identify the widow Alice (*Alys*, *Alisoun*), the Wife, of the Canterbury and many other pilgrimages. In *CT* A 445 she is referred to as "*of biside Bathe*", i.e., as living just outside the old town walls, specifically in the parish of St Michael's without the Walls or without North Gate. This identification was made by Richard Warner, *History of Bath* (Bath, 1801), pp. 360–61, on the basis of the miracle plays frequently put on in St Michael's church, today at the head of Northgate St (see below). This parish also specialized in weaving at which the Wife was adept. Manly 537; Bowden 214–15; Darby 251–53 and fig. 40. Elsewhere (*Buk* 29, *CT* D head., end and E 1170, 1685) she is merely "*of Bathe*", referred to in D 529 as "*our town*"; here just Bath in general is meant. Its former weaving importance is referred to in *CT* A 447 and the Wife's parish (of St Michael's) in A 448 with the church itself mentioned in D 593 and implied in D 629, where there was good preaching, the performance of miracle plays, and weddings (D 556, 559). The outskirts or open country are *feeldes* (D 548, 564). Muirhead *England* 151–52.

The name derives from the three mineral springs of the place, the only really hot springs in Britain, famous since Roman times when it was known as *Aquae Sulis* "waters sacred to (the Celtic female divinity) Sul", whom the Romans appear to have identified with Minerva; see Darby 54–55. In OE *hát baðu* "hot baths", *æt* (*þǽm hátum*) *báðum* "at (the hot) baths", the baths refer specifically to the Roman baths built there (adjoining the Pump Room in Stall St); since the seventeenth century the form of the name has been singular: "Bath." See *NED* "bath" sb. 2. Chaucer's form with *-e* presumably reflects the OE dat. plur. *baðum*.

Bel-Marye [var. MR V, 256] in effect corresponds to the present-day Morocco (*Marrok*) or *Al-Maghrib al-Aqsa* ("The Far West") of Arab geography and was in Chaucer's day the territory ruled by the Berber dynasty of the *Banu Marin* or Marinides "sons of Marin" (*E Isl* I, 464–66); the dynastic name is here extended to the territory, of which the chief town was

Tlemcen (*Tramissene*). *Bel-Marye* is mentioned in *CT* A 57 as a region where the Knight had fought (see also *Algezir* and Cook 228–29); in A 2630 it is a region abounding in fierce lions; for other North African lions, see *Libie*, below.

The dynastic name *Banu* or *Beni Marin* became distorted in OFr, perhaps by popular etymology, to *Belle-Marine, Bel-Marin, Belle-Mari* (see Cook 228, Manly 499 near end), whence into Middle English as in Chaucer, as *Bal-Meryne* in John Barbour's *Bruce* XX, 393, and as *Bel-More* in the *Sowdone of Babylone* 3122.

Berwyck [var. *Warrwik*, MR V, 65] is mentioned in a verse (*CT* A 692) apparently suggesting one limit of a stretch of territory within which the Pardoner had no equal in his profession (*craft*). The other limit is *Ware* (:*mare* "a mare") which may be either Ware (Herts) on the Lea and about 25 m. N of London (perhaps the more likely as the bigger and hence better-known town) or Ware, an east Kentish hamlet 3½ m. NW of Sandwich. But to identify Chaucer's *Berwyck* with any real certainty seems all but hopeless (cp. Manly 537), since Chaucer's form may be represented or reflected in almost any one of the thirteen modern Berwicks distributed among the counties of Essex, Kent, Northumberland, Shropshire, Sussex, Worcestershire, Yorkshire (West Riding), 3 Barwicks distributed among Norfolk Suffolk, Yorkshire (West Riding), 1 Berrick in Oxfordshire, and 1 Borwick in Lancashire. One most naturally thinks of Berwick-upon-Tweed (Northumberland) and the phrase "from Barwick to Dover, three hundred miles over" (Skeat V, 56 *ad loc.*) and thus, whichever Ware is meant, obtain a considerable distance or extensive territory within which Chaucer seems to want us to think of the Pardoner as operating. But he may be joking or anything.

The name looks back to OE *bere-wíċ* "grain farm".

Bethulia [Lat. *Betylua*], Bethulia, a far from certainly identified locality but perhaps to be associated with the town of Shechem or Sichem, later (Flavia) Neapolis, mod. Nab(u)lus(?), in ancient Samaria, corresponding to central Israel. In *CT* B *3755 (2565) it is a *strong cité* and a center of Isrealitish resistance to the Assyrian Nebuchadrezzar II; in B *2289 (1098) it is a *cité*, delivered by Judith from the hands of Nebuchadrezzar's general Holophernes.

For literature on this disputed name, see Robert H. Pfeiffer, *The History of New Testament Times, with an Introduction to the Apocrypha* (New York: Harper, 1949), p. 297, n. 15.

[under the] Blee(n) [var. MR VIII, 61, 142] "(in the lee of) the Blean Woods" (K), is mentioned in *CT* G 556 to define *Boghtoun* and in H 3 to define *Bobbe-Up-and-Doun*. Blean Wood(s), forming the NE part of an extensive forest belt which once covered the greater part of Kent, formerly commenced at Boughton (*Boghtoun*) and reached almost to the walls of Canterbury; it still crosses W of Canterbury through parts of Harbledown (see *Caunterbury Wey*). To the east there neither is now nor probably was in the past any woodland of consequence. This woodland, still the most extensive in Kent and formerly next in importance to the Weald, is now divided under various local names. See Robert Furley, *A History of the Weald of Kent*, etc., I (London, 1871), 389–90, 61–62; also Jerrold 90, 92, and J. K. Wallenberg, *Kentish Place-Names*, etc. (Uppsala Universitets Årsskrift, 1931), pp. 63–64.

The -*n* in the name Blean (ME *Bleen*) is evidently organic
and has been constant since Anglo-Saxon times (see Wallenberg 63 and *DEPN s.v.*) with the *n*-less forms chiefly in Chaucer
manuscripts where they are probably scribal. The name is of
uncertain origin, possibly connected with Welsh *blaen* "extremity, end, border" or with an OE weak dative singular *bléan
from *bléa "rough terrain".

Bobbe-Up-and-Doun [var. MR VIII, 142], "*a litel toun*"
mentioned in *CT* H 2 as being "*under the Blee, in Canterbury
Weye*", has been the subject of much discussion (Skeat V, 435,
n. 2; Robinson 763, n. 2). The fullest and really only thorough
examination of the locality and roads round about—made at
the request of Dr. Furnivall—is that by Cowper in 1868 (reprinted in Furnivall 32–34, later by Littlehales 36–38) who argues
strongly for identification with Up-and-Down Field at Cockering Farm in the parish of Thanington Without about 1 m. SW
of Canterbury and on the road on which *Boghtoun* in Chaucer's
day may quite possibly have stood. Cowper's statement deserves
respectful consideration. The alternative possibility, which I
am inclined to view as somewhat questionable, though it has
long been the popular view (but cp. Manly 654), is identification
with the small village of Harbledown set in a hillside (Littlehales 39, Jerrold 89–90) on the upper, main road leading into
Canterbury and, like Up-and-Down Field, about 1 m. outside
the town. See *Caunterbury Wey*, below. Erasmus' experience
at Harbledown (quoted by Littlehales 39 as a sort of clincher)
tells nothing about Chaucer's pilgrims but only what Erasmus,
and no doubt many Canterbury pilgrims, did. Cowper also
points out that nowhere else does Chaucer invent nicknames
of places or play with such words. And it might be remarked

that his *Bobbe-Up-and-Doun* bears little resemblance to Harble-down, a name which though unique (OE *Herebeald[es] dún* "Here-beald's hill") is not "funny" sounding, but that it is strikingly close to the name Up-and-Down Field which may in Chaucer's day actually have been known, jocosely or other-wise, in deference to the general undulating character of the countryside as *Bobbe-Up-and-Doun*. The name may indeed have referred to some tiny hamlet there. A bit of intensive work with the local records rather than further perambulations might do something to clear the matter up.

Boghtoun [**under Blee**, *q.v.*], answers formally to the pre-sent-day village of Boughton Street or Boughton under Blean (K) on the main Canterbury highway about 31/2 m. SE of Faversham and about 1 m. after the fork at Brentley Corner; it is mentioned in *CT* G 556 (var. MR VIII, 61) as near the spot where the disreputable canon and his yeoman overtake the pilgrims (see [*Ospringe*], below). If the present Boughton is on the site of Chaucer's *Boghtoun*, then *Bobbe-Up-and-Doun* is probably somehow to be identified with Harbledown, but there is considerable doubt whether such is the case. Much points to the name Boughton having applied in earlier times to the present hamlet of South Street about 3 m. from Ospringe or Faversham; see Cowper in Littlehales 36–38 and Littlehales 38–39; Robinson 15 'Frag. IX (Group H)'. The hamlet of South Street, it has been noted, is about 5 m. from Ospringe ([*Ospringe*]), a fact which fits the statement "*Er we hadde riden fully five miles*" (G 552) from the generally assumed Ospringe *hostelrye* of G 589; the present Boughton under Blean is only about 3½ m. from Ospringe. Something has been made of the fact that the South Street route into Canterbury is less direct than the northerly main road, but the facts presented above plus what can be said about *Bobbe-Up-and-Doun* speak for its being the route taken by Chaucer's pilgrims. See also *Caunterbury Wey*, below.

Early forms of the name: DB *Boltune*, 1247, 1288 *Bocton* make it uncertain whether the name looks back to OE *bóc-tún* "a *tún* where beeches grow" or to OE *bóþl-* or *bold-tún* "manor-house settlement", the latter usually the source of the name Bolton. Some English Boughtons look back to *Buccan-tún* "Bucca's *tún*". See *DEPN s.v.*

Boloigne:

I. [var. MR V, 42] in *CT* A 465 refers to Boulogne-sur-Mer (dép. Pas-de-Calais), France, one of the goals of the Wife's many pilgrimages; in this instance the specific reference would be to the cathedral church of Notre Dame in the so-called "Haute Ville", destroyed in the French Revolution and replaced by a modern structure. The harbor of Boulogne is the Roman *Gaesoriacus* (Holder I, 1512–13), later *Boninia* (*Bunne* of the *Anglo-Saxon Chronicle*). It may be noted that Boulogne-sur-Gesse (Haute-Garonne) was named after *Boloigne* II; see Longnon No. 2459. Boulogne is still a middle-class English week-end tourist attraction.

II. (var. MR VI, 353, 369) Bologna, Italy, on the edge of the Emilian plain (see *Emele*) some 50 m. N of Florence, is mentioned in *CT* E 686, 763, 939, 1069, as the home of the Count of Panico (*Erl of Panyk*), brother-in-law of Marquis Walter of *Saluces* and the town where for years Walter kept his and Griselde's daughter and son (*EI* VII, 329–31, and see also *Panyk*).

The name of both the French and Italian town looks back to Celto-Lat. *Bononia* (Holder I, 482–87), both later yielding

by dissimilation *Bolonia*, whence respectively Fr. *Boulogne* and
Ital. *Bologna*. See Matthias 66–68 for late survivals in German
of the type *Bononie* vs *Bolonie*.

Bowe, see **Stratford-atte-Bowe.**

brasile, brazil, more commonly brazil wood, was the name
first applied in western Europe in the late eleventh and early
twelfth centuries (Caetano da Silva, *cit. infra*, pp. 6, 9, 11, 12)
to a small thorny tree or shrub with yellow blossoms native
to Malaya, the *Caesalpinia sappan*, Malay *sapang*, English *sapan*
or *sapan* wood (*NED s.v.*), whose wood properly treated yields
a brilliant red dye; in time the word came to be used for the
dye itself with the essential element brazilin. See Daniel V.
Thompson, *The Materials of Mediaeval Painting* (London,
1936), pp. 116–21, also Thompson and George H. Hamilton,
*An Anonymous Fourteenth-Century Treatise "De Arte Illumi-
nandi"* etc. (New Haven, Conn., 1933), pp. 8–9, 44–45, nn.
77–79. Later the name was transferred to a related dyewood
tree of the same family, the *Caesalpinia echinata*, discovered in
South America by the Portuguese, who were already familiar
with the East Indian plant in which they had long traded. The
land in the New World where it was discovered was first known
as Terra de Santa Cruz but early referred to familiarly as Terra
do Brazil; see F. Assis Cintra, *O Nome "Brasil" (com S ou com
Z)* (São Paulo, Brazil, 1921), *passim*, also John B. Stetson, Jr.,
transl., *The Histories of Brazil by Pero de Magalhães* (New York:
Cortes Society, 1922), II, 194–95, n. 14; there is a generous
listing of early documents with various forms of the name of
the dyewood in Joaquim Caetano da Silva, 'Questões Ameri-
canas ... Brazil', *Revista Trimensal do Instituto Historico, Geo-*

graphico e Ethnographico do Brazil, XXIX (Rio de Janeiro, 1866), pt ii, pp. 5–35 (wrongly cited by Stetson). The principal source of commercial brazil wood used today in the United States is, however, the Central American tree *Haematoxylon brasiletto*, whose dye is used to a very limited extent in wool and calico printing and formerly in the manufacture of red ink. On all this, see Isaac H. Burkill, *A Dictionary of the Economic Products of the Malay Peninsula* I (London, 1935), 390–91; Samuel J. Record and Robert W. Hess, *Timbers of the New World* (New Haven, Conn., 1943), p. 239; John Hutchinson and Ronald Melville, *The Story of Plants and their Uses to Man* (London: Gawthorn, 1948), pp. 241–42, 244 (colored plate). For these and other botanical references I am most grateful to Dr. Richard E. Schultes of Harvard University.

Brasile is mentioned in *CT* B² *4649 (3459) in the verse: *With brasile and with greyn of Portyngale* (without the editors' comma after *brasile*) (a passage cited in Portuguese translation in Caetano da Silva, p. 7; in English by Cintra, p. 31), where along with *greyn* (see *Portyngale*) its brilliant red is mentioned to imply the complexion of the Nun's Priest. There is every reason here to think of Portugal as the exporting country of the brazil wood as well as of the kermes or "grain", especially since the Portuguese are known to have traded in this dyewood (Hutchinson and Melville, p. 242).

For the etymology of *brasile* and, consequently, of the name of the South American country many suggestions have been put forward, often insubstantial; see "Analyse e Critica das Diversas Hypotheses" in Cintra, pp. 103–87, summarized pp. 8–9, to which add an elaborate and unconvincing suggestion by Leo Wiener in Stetson II, 195–203. The East Indian (Malay) name, as noted above, is *sapang* and the like, the Arabic name is *baqqam* of unknown origin (not *braza* as Hutchinson and Melville, p. 242); thus the Orient does not seem to be the promising source of the name as suggested by *NED* s.v. "brasil", headnote, and M-L 1st ed., 1911, No. 1277 "*brasile", an entry cancelled in the 3d ed. The currently accepted, though to me semantically somewhat dubious etymology bases the word on a Romanic **brasa* "live, red-hot coal", yielding northern Ital. *braza*, whence Span. *brasa*, Port. *braza*, OFr *breze*, Fr. *braise*, etc. (M-L No. 1276 "brasa") plus the Latin suffix *-ilis* "having the quality of". This Romanic **brasa* is in turn presumed to look back to a Germanic **brasa* of similar meaning, represented in Swed. *brasa* "fire, blaze", Norw. *brase* "to burn". The first to propose an etymology for *brazil wood/Brazil* based on the Port. common noun *braza* appears to have been Pedro (Pero) de Magalhães de Gandavo, *Historia de Provincia de Santa Cruz a que vulgarmente chamamos Brasil*, etc. (Lisbon, 1576), chap. 1 *ad fin*, fol. 7^v (see Stetson, *op. cit.*, I [facsimile], fol. 7^v; II, 23 [translation]). A similar etymology is given by Du Cange *s.v.* "brasile", and others, including perhaps most recently Oscar Bloch and Walther von Wartburg, *Dictionnaire étymologique de la langue française* (Paris: Presses Universitaires, 1950), *s.v.* "braise". Elof Hellquist, *Svensk etymologisk Ordbok* (2d ed., Lund, 1939), *s.v.* "bresilje", mentions this etymology only as a possibility and I consider his caution justified.

Bret, adj. British, is used in *HF* 1208 (3, 118) to define an unidentified Welsh bard Glascurion (Robinson 784, col. 2–785, col. 1, n. 1208).

The adjective looks back to OE *Bret* (plur. *Brettas*) "Briton"; see *NED* "Brit" sb. 2 (and § *a*).

Britai(g)ne (Briteyne) Britain:

I. Great Britain, mentioned in *CT* A 409 as a region of which the Shipman knew every little arm of the sea suitable for loading or unloading small vessels ("*cryke*", *CT* A 408; *NED* "creek" sb. 1). In *CT* F 810 it is identified with England (see *Engelond*, below).

II. Brittany, France, in Chaucer's day a dukedom of the house of Montfort, embracing the modern departments of Côtes-du-Nord, Finistère, Ille-et-Vilaine, Loire Inférieure, and Morbihan. Mentioned in *CT* F 729, it is equated with the older (Classical-Celtic) name of the region "Amorica" (*Armorik*), this latter being used in F 1061 adjectivally (*Armorik Briteyne*) to distinguish it from "Great" Britain (I, above). It is also mentioned in F 992, 1159, 1221, 1240, 1268; these references all apply to the maritime zone of Brittany and specifically to the district (*contré*, F 800) centering on the commune of Penmarc'h (*Pedmark*) in F 801 (in F 1351, 1502 a *toun*) in the SW corner of Finistère, home of "Arveragus of Kayrrud" (F 808 and probably with reference to some one of the common Breton place-names "Kerru" = Welsh Caerudd). Consonant with the subject of the Franklin's Tale great stress is laid upon the reef-filled sea and rock-bound coast, dangerous then as now to sailing craft. The *see* off the coast is mentioned in F 847, 863, 896, and the rocks in F 859, 868, 891, 993, 1061, 1064, 1158, 1221, 1268, 1296, 1301, 1338. On these rocks and the hazardous shore-line see John S. P. Tatlock, *The Scene of the Franklin's Tale Visited* (Chaucer Society, Second Ser. 51, London, 1914), pp. 1–9, and for an excellent modern description by a yachtsman see Frank Cowper, *Sailing Tours*, etc. Part III, *The Coast of Brittany*, etc. (London, 1894), pp. 156–58, also Claud Worth,

Yacht Cruising (2d ed., London, 1921), p. 200, with a splendid chart facing p. 107.

See Gröhler II, 9; Holder I, 603, 604–09.

Brito(u)n, sb.—adj. Briton, Breton.

I. 1. sb. a native of Great Britain, in Chaucer always referring to pre-Saxon or Celtic Britain and virtually equivalent to "Welsh"; see *NED* "Briton": so in *CT* B 545, 547, 561, with reference to members of the pre-Saxon British church. Cp. *Bret*, above.

2. adj. a "*Britoun book*" (B 666) refers ostensibly to a copy of the early Welsh Gospels (*Evaungiles*).

II. 1. sb. plur. natives of "Lesser Britain", Brittany, France, are mentioned in *CT* F 707 as producers of poems or lays and in D 858 perhaps as a people much interested in King Arthur. In F 1179 it is the nationality of Aurelius' scholar-brother (*clerk*, F 1105).

2. adj. *Briton tonge* "Breton language" is mentioned in F 711 as the language of native Breton lays (cp. II, 1, above).

Bromeholm, Bromholm Priory, a ruin, especially a Norman gatehouse in a farm-yard at Bacton (Nf), a coast-guard station 4 1/2 m. NE of North Walsham (Nf), is used in *CT* A 4286 (var. MR V, 422) by Symond the miller's wife as part of an oath "*Holy Croys of B.*" with reference to the Cross or Rood of Bromholm in the Cluniac Bromholm Priory founded in 1113, also mentioned in *Piers Plowman B*, V, 231: *And bidde the Rode of Bromeholme brynge me oute of dette* (Skeat *PPl* II, 84–5, n.); see R. A. Pratt, 'Chaucer and the Holy Cross of Bromholm', *Mod. Lang. Notes* LXX (1955), 324–25. Muirhead *England* 613.

The name is based on OE *bróm* m. "broom plant" and ON

hólmr "islet", "isolated piece of ground characterized by a growth of broom".

Brugges [var. often *Brigges*, MR VII, 115, 116, 133, 138, 185], Du. Brugge or Fr. Bruges, West Flanders, Belgium, about 6 m. from the coast, was accessible from the North Sea until the final silting up of the Zwijn in 1490. *Brugges* did much wool-trading with England and in banking was the nothern counter-part of Venice in the south. In *CT* B² *1245 (55) where it is a *toun*, *1251 (61), *1448 (258), *1491 (301) it is the goal of a sum-mer business trip by a French banker of *Seint-Denys*, where he appears to attend strictly to business and no nonsense. (B² *1492–96 [302–06].) In B² *1923 (733) *Brugges* defines Sir Tho-pas' brown hose. See also *Flaundryssh*.

The name, of uncertain origin and meaning, was early asso-ciated with Du. *brug* "bridge" (cp. OE *Brycg* in the *Anglo-Saxon Chronicle*) and was evidently so understood; see *NGF* III, 28, and cp. Gröhler II, 187.

Burdeux [var. MR VII, 67], Bordeaux on the Garonne (dép. Gironde [*Gerounde*]) in Chaucer's day belonged, if somewhat tenuously, to England along with Aquitaine. Commerce be-tween Bordeaux and England was exceedingly active, not least that dealing with fine wines of the region. It is mentioned as a source of wine in *CT* A 397, C 571 (where it is a *toun*), in the latter instance with the strong suggestion that the wines of Bordeaux and La Rochelle (*The Rochele*) were being challenged in popularity with the stronger Spanish wines of *Lepe*.

The name looks back to Rom. (Iberian?) *Burdigala* (Holder I, 633–37), later *Burdegala*, OFr *Bordele*, later *Bordeux*; see Gröh-ler I, 64–65. For *Bordeuz*, even *Burdegale*, of very different ori-gin see Gröhler II, 260; Longnon No. 2708.

Burgoyne, the old French duchy of Lower Burgundy [Fr. *Bourgogne*] with Dijon as its capital, is mentioned in *RR* 554 (not in *Roman de la Rose* 542), where "*Fro Jerusalem into Burgoyne*" expresses a great distance within which no girl had a neck fairer than Ydelnesse (*RR* 593).

Like *Fraunce* itself the name is Germanic, Med. Lat. *Burgundia*, whence the French and Chaucer's form (Gröhler II, 4–5); the ethnic name *Burgundiones* survives in the Fr. adj. *bourguignon* "Burgundian" (Longnon No. 535). The original home of the Burgundians seems to have been on the Danish island of Bornholm in the Baltic, ON *Burgundarholmr* "island of the Burgundians" and OE *Burgenda land* of similar meaning; see further *Reallexikon* I, 357–58.

C

Calydoigne clearly reflects an OFr *Calidoi(g)ne*, in turn looking back to non-classical **Calydonia*, and thus would mean "region centering on Calydon" (Lat. *Calydon*), perhaps falsely inferred from *Calydonia regna* of Ovid's *Met.* 15, 769, describing the realm of Diomedes in Apulia, Italy, whither he is said to have gone after the fall of Troy. Really intended by Chaucer is, however, the ancient Aetolian town on the lower reaches of the Euenus (now Phidaris); the town gave its name to the Gulf of Calydon (now Gulf of Patras, Patrai). Said to have been founded by Calydon, son of Aetolus, eponym of Aetolia, it was the royal residence of Oeneus, father of Meleager and Deianira and grandfather of Diomedes. *Calydoigne* occurs only with a following *and Arge* (i.e., Argos) to describe in *TC* 5, 805 the kingdom of Tydeus of Aetolia to which Diomedes is heir (*TC* 5, 934).

Campayne, ancient Roman province of Campania, south of Latium, of which the chief city was Capua and famed for its fertility, is mentioned in *Bo* 1, pr. 4, l. 97 (120–25) as the *provynce of Campayne* in connection with measures once taken by Boethius himself in a time of famine.

This region is not to be associated with the well-known modern "Campagna" surrounding Rome.

Cananee, adj. Cananaean, Canaanitic, of or pertaining to the land of Canaan [Lat. *Chanaanaeus*], is used in *CT* G 59 in connection with the story of the woman of Canaan (*mulier Chanaanaeae*, *Matth.* xv, 22). The adjective looks back to the ancient regional name Canaan, more commonly Land of Canaan (*terra Chanaan*), generally denoting the low-lying part of Israel west of the Jordan and the Dead Sea.

Canaan, fourth son of Ham, is mentioned in *CT* I 765.

[The] Cane [of Galilee], Cana [Lat. *Cana*], a not certainly identified locality in Galilee, mentioned in *CT* D 11 with reference to the wedding in Cana (*John* ii, 1). The phrasal formula follows the original *in Cana Galilaeae*; I do not understand the use of the definite article since there seems to be no other Cana's in the Bible. The locality is either to be identified with mod. Kefr-Kenna *ca* 4 m. NNE of Nazareth or, perhaps less likely —since there is no spring there—with Khirbet Kana 9 m. N of Nazareth.

Canterbregge, Cambridge [var. MR V, 389, 395] on the Cam, county town with full-fledged university since at least 1209, is mentioned in *CT* A 3921 as not far from *Trumpington* and in A 3990 as the site of *Soler Halle*. Muirhead *England* 568–81.

The present name has developed irregularly from OE *Grantanbrycg* (cp. the near-by village of Grantchester SW of Cambridge) and meant "bridge over the *Grante*", now Cam, a late back-formation from the present town name. *PN* XIX *C* 2–3 ("Cam"), 36–38 ("Cambridge").

Caribdis, Charybdis [Lat. *Charybdis*], legendarily a dangerous whirlpool in later classical times located on the Sicilian side of the Straits of Messina opposite Scylla which was placed on the Italian side. In *TC* 5, 644 Charybdis threatens, figuratively speaking, to destroy Troilus and his ship (of life); in *RR* 4713 it is used, as in classical tradition, of anything dangerous or destructive: love is a *Caribdis* (var. *Karibdous*) *perilous*.

Carre Nar, Qara Na'ur or Nur "Black Lake", on the eastern side of the Gobi (*Drye See*), Outer Mongolia, is mentioned in *BD* 1029 as a point on the route across the *Drye See* to which the Duchess of Lancaster would not have sent an admirer on an irksome or futile mission (so *Alysaundre*, *Drye See*, *Pruyce*, *Tartarye* I, *Turkye*, *Walakye*). See Lowes *passim*.

The name is Mongolian, looking back to *Naghur* > *Na'ur* > *Nūr*, the latter often approximating *Nōr* in pronunciation. Chaucer's form *Nar* seems to be more closely related to the type *Na'ur* the *Nōr's* (cited and discussed by Lowes, esp. 19–21) to *Nūr*, though there is no particular reason to view Chaucer's form as suspect or in need of extensive explanation.

I. **Cartage,** Carthage [Lat. *Kartago*, *-inis*], ancient Phoenician colonial city on the north-east coast of Africa near the mod. city of Tunis in the district of Tunis, was founded *ca* 850 B.C. by refugees from Tyre, led by Ellis(s)a(r), daughter of King Beleus of Tyre; Elissar is better known by her later epithet "Dido", "the refugee". After a long and brilliant history Byrsa, the citadel, was dismantled by P. Scipio Africanus in 146 B.C. at the end of the Third Punic War.

Cartage is used to define Dido's queenship (*BD* 732, *LGW* 1283) and as a symbol of great wealth (*BD* 1062, cp. 1060). It is a *cité* (*LGW* 1049, 1051), a *toun* (*LGW* 1016, *CT* F 1401), a *faire toun* (*HF* 432), *noble toun of Cartage* (*LGW* 1008), and as the place to which Venus directs Aeneas (*HF* 236, *LGW* 1000) to seek out the survivors among his shipwrecked comrades (cp. *BD* 209–10, 220–21, 237–38; *LGW* 902). The outlying region of Libya is referred to as the *contré of Cartage* (*HF* 224); on certain aspects of this Libyan countryside see *Affrike*, above, and *Libie*, below. Aeneas takes refuge in the *haven* (*LGW* 963), perhaps to be imagined as the ancient military harbor of Cothon. A *temple*, meeting-place of Aeneas and Dido (cp. Troilus and Criseyde under *Troie*, below), is featured in *LGW* 1024, 1036, 1052, 1270; it is large (*LGW* 1019), and in 1016 where it is referred to as the *mayster-temple* "main temple", it is perhaps appropriately to be conceived of historically as the famous temple of Tanit (Phoenician Astarte, Roman Venus), palladium of Carthage.

Dido's *royal paleys* (*LGW* 1096) is luxuriously appointed and has richly hung ball-rooms (*LGW* 1106: *dauncynge chaumbers ful of paramentes*); her apartment (*chaumbre*) is mentioned in *HF* 366, Aeneas' in *LGW* 1111. One or the other or both these suites of rooms are the site of the action of much of the later part of the story in *LGW*. There is a courtyard (*LGW* 1194: *court*) outside the royal palace. Out in the forested countryside (see *Libie*, below) is a *(litel) cave* (*LGW* 1125, 1244), somewhat central to the action of the story and source of court scandal (*LGW* 1242: *wikke fame*).

The destruction of Carthage by the Romans is alluded to in *CT* B *4555 (3365) and in F 1400, the latter with specific reference to the suicide of the wife of Hasdrubal, last-ditch defender of Carthaginian freedom. The impending destruction of the city is portended in *PF* 44 (cp. l. 37), where Scipio Africanus in 150 B.C. visits Massinissa, king of Numida.

In *LGW* 1188 *se* might be imagined historically as the Gulf of Carthage or the Lake of Tunis.

II. **Cartage** Cartagena (prov. Murcia), Spain, Mediterranean seaport, is mentioned in *CT* A 404 as the southern limit of a stretch of water and coastline, of which *Hulle* is the northern, with which the Shipman is intimately familiar.

The name looks back to its Roman name *Carthago* (*Nova*) (see *Cartage* I, for the ancient African city). Chaucer's form, based on the nominative case, is a common OFr form of what is modern Fr. *Carthagène* and in thus homonymous with his name of the ancient city. The Spanish form in *-ena* presumably reflects the Lat. oblique cases *Carthagīn-* with long, accented *i*.

Cataloigne, Catalonia [Catal. *Catalunya*, Span. *Cataluña*, Fr. *Catalogne*], S of the Pyrenees and just E of *Aragon* with which it formed in Chaucer's day a joint kingdom, is mentioned along with *Aragon* in *HF* 1248 (3, 158) as a land notable for its trumpet- and clarion-players, on which see under *Aragon*.

The name, appearing in Med. Lat. as *Catalonia*, is of much discussed etymology with often fanciful proposals. It may well look back to Lat. *castellanus* "guardian of lands or castles", yielding Catal. *ca(s)tlán > catalán* with the suffix *-ia* yielding *Catalunya* "land of guardians of castles"; cp. OFr *chastelain*, Fr. *châtelain*, and see *EUI* XII, 464–65. Chaucer's form is from OFr *Cateloi(g)ne*.

Caucasus [**Kaukasous**], the mountain system of the Caucasus (Lat. *Caucasus*) between the Black and the Caspian Seas, is mentioned in *Bo* 2, pr. 7, l. 71 (540–45) as a *mountaigne* which in the time of Cicero (106–43 B.C.) had not yet come under Roman sway. In *CT* D 1140 it is the *mount of Kaukasous*, mentioned as a very remote region and used as a figure of great distance (cp. *Inde*, below). With the use here of *montaigne* and *mount* in the singular for a whole mountain-range, cp. OE *munt* for the Alps and OE *mór* for the Kjöllen range in Norway.

Caunterbury [var. *Cauntourbyri*, MR V, 73], Canterbury (K) on the Stour, county town with cathedral, now the archepiscopal see of the Primate of All England, is mentioned in *CT* A 16–17, 769–770, as the site of the shrine of St Thomas, of Norman parentage and known as Becket, also there and as follows for the town itself: *CT* A 22, 27, 793 (*to-Caunterbury-ward*), 801, G 624 (*C. toun*). The shrine of St Thomas, goal of the pilgrims and in Chaucer's day of incredible richness (Manly 496), was in the Trinity Chapel behind the high altar of the cathedral but was destroyed in 1538 and the saint's remains burned (see *DNB* XIX, 650, cols 1–2; Muirhead *England* 28). The shrine is referred to in terms of the saint (*martir*) in *CT* A 16–17, 769–770, and his name invoked in A 3291, 3425, 3461, D 666, 2107, *HF* 1131 (3, 41).

In *CT* I 1086 it describes or refers to the Tales: *the Tales of C., th'ilke sounen into sinne*. The title or phrase *Tales of C.* or "The Canterbury Tales", today the common designation, deserves a word of comment; on the early history of these titles see Aage Brusendorff, *The Chaucer Tradition* (London–Copenhagen, 1925), pp. 134–36. Neither Chaucer's nor the modern phrase really mean anything in ordinary English, since such a title ought to mean either "tales told in Canterbury" (cp. Henry W. Longfellow's *Tales of a Wayside Inn*) or "tales about the town of Canterbury". Yet obviously the title means neither but rather "tales told by pilgrims en route to and/or from Canterbury". We seem here to have an example of the phenomenon of the dropping—in reality or by implication—of the middle link of a three-link compound, that is, as if *Canterbury Tales* stood for *Canterbury Pilgrims' Tales*—which is just what they are. With this compare the almost classic examples of in any literal sense meaningless Germ. *Sonn-abend* and OE *Sunnan-áfen* "Sun-eve" or "Day before the Sun", each standing however for *Sonn-tags-abend* and *Sunnan-dæges áfen* "Eve of or Day before Sunday". On this see Otto Ritter, *Vermischte Beiträge zur englischen Sprachgeschichte*, etc. (Halle, 1922), pp. 88–90, Gustav Stern, *Meaning and Change of Meaning* (Göteborgs Högskolas Årsskrift, XXXVIII, 1932, No. 1), pp. 276–77, and on certain broader implications George K. Zipf, *The Psycho-Biology of Language* (Boston, 1935), Index, under "Abbreviatory Truncation".

The name is based on the OE dat.-loc. sing. (*æt*, *on*, *to* etc.) *Cant-wara-byriʒ* "(at, in, to etc.) the fortified place of the people of Kent (Celtic *Kantion*)". It may be noted that the mediaeval and modern French equivalent *Cantorbéri* derives from the Old-Kentish form *Cant-wara-beriʒ*, with its typical southeastern *e* for *y*.

Caunterbury Wey, "Canterbury Highway", essentially the present-day Route A2, the old Roman Watling-Street (see *Watlynge-Strete*, below), has also been known as the Dover Road and the Old Kent(ish) Road; stretches of the route have here and there local designations; the distance from Southwark to Canterbury has been reckoned as 56–57 m. (Tatlock 481). The route is mentioned in *CT* H 3 and is implied in the set phrase *by the weye* in *CT* A 771, 774, 780, 806, 834, D 1274. On the route in mediaeval times in general and in connection with Chaucer's pilgrims in particular, see Furnivall, Littlehales, Tatlock, and Owen. For maps of the mediaeval route see Littlehales, also Manly facing p. 494.

In the following discussion of the *Caunterbury Wey* the names are presented in their proper geographical order, though this order occurs fully in no *CT* manuscript; the most striking violation of geographical order comes as a result of the notorious manuscript separation of Groups B¹ (II) and B² (VII), whereby *Rouchestre* of B *3116 (1926) comes after *Sidyngborne* of D 847 (MR II, 491–92). Included in the main list of names and referred to in the present entry below are [*Derteford*] and [*Ospringe*], though these are not mentioned by Chaucer. The reason for their inclusion—as possible overnight stops—is discussed under the names themselves and summarily at the end of the present entry. It is somehow unsatisfying to deal with the *Caunterbury Wey* without some consideration—however futile such discussion surely is—of the number of days Chaucer might have assigned to the journey, had he developed his grand project to that point, in a word, to a discussion of possible or likely overnight stops.

In the main the pilgrims probably followed the course of the old Roman Watling-Street but at certain points may well have departed from it, for there were here and there alternate routes and not all pilgrims necessarily chose the same. In such cases one is reduced to a consideration of possibilities which can never be converted into certainties.

The pilgrims may be assumed to have got out of the London

area from the Tabard Inn in Southwark (*Southwerk*) by riding down the Borough High Street (S.E.1), and Great Dover Street (S.E.1.), Old Kent(ish) Road (S.E.1.) close to whose second mile-stone was a spring or brook, St Thomas' Watering, S.E.1 (*Wateryng of Seint Thomas*), on and out New Cross Road (S.E.14) to Deptford, S.E.8 (*Depeford*) (Littlehales 10). At Deptford they would naturally have turned into Blackheath Road and up to Blackheath Hill, though probably skirting the side of Green- wich Park, S.E.10 (*Grenewych*), rather than following the pre- sent main road across the heath (Littlehales 11). Then it would be back up on the "Old" Dover Road to the main highway on to Shooter's Hill by Eltham Common (S.E.9) and on to Welling and Bexleyheath, Kent. At this point the present road is appa- rently not the old road (in existence until 1796, Littlehales 12). Then on to Crayford (K) where, at the local gas-works, there may have been at that time as now two roads available to pass through the town, Old Road and London Road, both at the foot of the High Street joining Crayford Road leading to Dart- fort (K) (*Derteford*) about 15 m. from Southwark. Though not mentioned in *CT*, it is possible that Chaucer would have made Dartford the first overnight stop (see below).

Proceeding out of Dartford and over the top of the hill to a small heath called Dartford Brent (Jerrold 377) there is again a choice of roads leading to Strood–Rochester (*Rouchestre*), some 15 m. beyond Dartford and 30 m. from Southwark. The main road is the left fork and passes Stone, Gravesend, and Gadshill; the more direct Roman road goes straight on. Available evidence concerning the route ordinarily taken by Canterbury pilgrims favors, however, the main road via Gravesend (Littlehales 17– 23). Strood (Intra and Extra; OE *stród* "marshy land overgrown with brushwood"), reached by either road, stands across the

Medway from Rochester and Chatham, with which it was in Chaucer's day joined by a stone bridge (Littlehales 25–26). Under another dispensation the pilgrims might have spent the night there. For some distance beyond Rochester the route is plain enough (Littlehales 26–32): the pilgrims would go through Chatham and on to Sittingbourne (*Sidyngborne*), then pass Bapchild 1½ m. farther on and a bit over 17 m. beyond Rochester have come to Ospringe (*Ospringe*) 1½ m. SW of Faversham and about 10 m. NW of Canterbury (Littlehales 34–35); it is virtually certain that we should think of them as spending the night here. On what may most reasonably be viewed as the last day of the journey to Canterbury the pilgrims set out on the final short stretch of the way; it cannot be completely ruled out, however, that we may have here to do with the return trip to Southwark.

At Brenley Corner (Littlehales 36), about 2 m. beyond Faversham–Ospringe, the highway forks, both forks leading to Canterbury, a little over 9 m. from Ospringe. The main and apparently normal and most direct pilgrim, and modern automobile, route was the left or north fork (Watling-Street, London Road— Route A2), but which of these alternate routes Chaucer had in mind has been the subject of discussion. The weight of evidence (not the number of voices) seems to me to favor rather strongly the right or south fork, with *Boghtoun-under-Blee* (Littlehales 38–39) referring in those days to the locality now known as South Street; in this event *Bobbe-Up-and-Doun* is perhaps to be viewed as once the name of a tiny hamlet in the area of the present Up-and-Down Field at Cockering Farm in the parish of Thanington Without, stretching along the Canterbury and Ashford Road (Route A28). If this is the route, the pilgrims would have proceeded along Thanington Road, Wincheap,

Castle Street, St Margaret's Lane, and Mercery Lane to the Cathedral. If they took the upper or north fork and passed Harbledown, then they would follow London Road to St Dunstan's Church, thence to the Cathedral. Today St Margaret's Street is a one-way street toward Thanington, so the route described can only be taken by car in an out-of-town direction. Driving into Canterbury by way of Thanington one must follow Wincheap, then Pin Hill, Rhodaus Town, Upper Bridge Street, St George's Street, then Mercery Lane.

There has been much discussion about possible overnight stops that the pilgrims might have made, had they made them. The basis of modern scholarly discussion is that by Furnivall (pp. 12–17) with the upshot-with which many scholars have agreed—that there were three places with suitable sleeping accommodations on the road, at each one of which the pilgrims should be imagined as having spent the night: Dartford (p. 19), Rochester (p. 22), and Ospringe (p. 29), thus reaching Canterbury some time in the course of the fourth day; see his tabular view, pp. 42–43 (reprinted in Littlehales 40–44). Perhaps rightly— Tatlock 485, n. 1 seems to be more charitable—Furnivall (pp. 15–17, [145] "Corrections and Additions") took a dim view of the state of the road and wanted the pilgrims to cover no more than 15 or 16 m. per day; yet see Darby 260–62, 261, nn. 1–2. This schedule or time table was generally accepted (Tatlock 478, n. 4) until Tatlock came out for a three-day journey (Tatlock 483) with overnight stops at Dartford (pp. 483, 484) and Ospringe (p. 484) but not at Rochester (pp. 483–84). Miss Rickert personally strongly favored a two-day trip each way (MR II, 493) but in MR II, 493–94, she or she and Manly (it is hard to know just whose opinion is being expressed) seem to have thought or recognized that a pilgrimage to Canterbury must have been planned for either three or four days. This Furnivall–Skeat scheme Lawrence (esp. 118) seems to accept. On the basis of a rather drastic rearrangement of the fragments Owen urges a five-day trip, of which three are to Canterbury and the fourth and fifth on the road back to Southwark (Owen 822–23 for a tabular view). This Pratt (1159, n. 35a) rejects without, however—as lying outside the scope of his paper—favoring any particular system of stops. As MR II, 493–94, rightly observe: "But certainly the question of the number of days occupied by the pilgrimage is a matter of very small consequence, since the whole conception of a series of tales told while riding by so large a group of pilgrims is, however entertaining, entirely unrealistic."

Chaldeye, Chaldaea [Lat. *Chaldaea*], in ancient geography a part of the Assyrian Empire at the head of the Persian Gulf (mod. Iraq), is mentioned in *CT* B *3347 (2157) as a part of the Assyrian empire of Nebuchadressar (*regn.* 605–562 B.C.) where no scholar but Daniel could be found to interpret the king's dreams. (Cp. *Dan.* v, 10–13.)

chalon [var. *clothes*, MR V, 410], a sort of fabric, is here probably a blanket manufactured or of the type manufactured in Châlons-sur-Marne (dép. Marne), France, which along with *sheetes* is mentioned in the plural in *CT* A 4140 as part of the covering of a bed made up by the miller Symond for the Cambridge students Alain and John.

See Jean Bonnard and Amédée Salmon, edd., Frédéric Godefroy, *Lexique de l'ancien français* (Paris–Leipzig, 1901), *s.v.* "chalun", Du Cange II, 303, col. 1, *s.v.* "chaluns", and p. 302, col. 2, *s.vv.* "chalo", "chalonus"; *NED s.v.* "chalon" and *s.v.*

"shalloon" for a later borrowing of the same word. From OFr the word also passed into MHG as *schalûne*.

The place-name *Châlons*, whence the common noun, looks back to the Gaulish tribal name *Catu-vellauni* "good, competent warriors" or the like; Merovingian *Catalaunis* yielded successively *Chaðelons*, *Chaelons*, modern *Châlons*; see Holder I, 863–65; Gröhler I, 88; Longnon No. 411.

Cilenios, -us, adj. Cyllenian, of or pertaining to Mt Cyllene in NE Arcadia (*Arcayde*, above), legendary birth-place of the god Mercury (Gk *Hermes*), whence the adjective also means "of or pertaining to Mercury". It is used for the god in *Mars* 113, 144, as a substantive "the one of Mt Cyllene".

Cymerie, Cimmeria [Lat. *Cimmeria*], legendary land of the Cimmerians (Lat. *Cimmerii*); historically the Cimmerians were driven out of their homeland in Thrace (*Trace*, below) by the Scythians (cp. *Scithie*, below) a little before the time of Homer and to the region of the Crimea: they are best known from the legendary description in *Odyssey* viii, 1 ff., where they are pictured as living in caves and in perpetual darkness, enshrouded in fog. It is in line with this tradition that a branch of the Lethe (*Lete*, below) is in *HF* 73 placed in their country, also thought of as the home of Morpheus, god of sleep.

Cipre, Ciprus, the island of Cyprus [Lat. *Cyprus*], formerly a British Crown Colony, now a republic in the eastern Mediterranean, off the Gulf of Iskanderun, formerly Alexandretta, in Turkey in Asia, was famed in antiquity for its copper mines and the cult of Venus; it is mentioned in *CT* B² *3581 (2391)— and in Lat. *de Cipro* in the preceding heading—as the kingdom of Pierre de Lusignan (d. 1369). On other of Pierre's campaigns in which the Knight is said to have taken part see *Alysaundre*, *Lyeys*, *Satalye*.

Graeco-Lat. *Cyprus* of disputed etymology has given its name to the element copper (Lat. *Cyprium aes* "Cyprian metal", later *cyprum*); see *NED s.v.* "copper". Chaucer's *Cipre* is OFr, modern Fr. (*île de*) *Chypre*.

Cipris, Cipride [Lat. *Cypris, -idis*], a Cypriot, earlier Cyprian. Here the Cypriot *par excellence*, Venus, is mentioned as *Cipris* in *HF* 518 (2, 10), *TC* 3, 725, as *Cipride* in *PF* 277, 652 (var. to *Cupide*), *TC* 4, 1216, 5, 208; see further *Cipre*.

The form *Cipris* is Latin, *Cipride* OFr and based on the Latin oblique cases.

Ciprus, see **Cipre.**

Cir[r]ea, [Lat. *Cirr(h)a*], properly a town in Phocis on the Gulf of Crisa, mod. Amphissa (off the Gulf of Corinth); inland and some 5 or 6 m. SSW of Mt Parnassus and Delphi (*Delphos*, below) was the ancient city of Crisa. By the ancients the name of the more important seaport Cirrha was often substituted for Crisa and it is for Crisa that Chaucer intends his *Cirrea*. It is mentioned more or less rightly in *Anel* 17 as not far from Mt Parnassus (*Parnaso*, below) and wrongly as near Mt Helicon (*Elicon*, below) some 25 m. away in Boeotia, whence it is said to be the home of the muse Poly(hy)mnia.

Formally Chaucer's *Cirrea* seems to show contamination of Lat. *Cirrha* by the adj. *Cirrhaeus* "of or pertaining to Cirrha".

Cithe, Cithia, see **Scithia,** below.

Cithero[u]n [Mount of], [Lat. *Cithaeron, -onis* m.], a mountain range, famous in Greek mythology as sacred to Bacchus and the Muses; now renamed from its pine forests it is called Elatia (Gk *elates* "silver fir"), separating Boeotia from Megaris and Attica, and on its northern slope is Plataea. In *CT* A 1936–38 the mountain is said to be represented by a mural in Venus' oratory, located over the east entry of the Theseus Bowl (see under *Attenes*, above), in A 2223 it is associated with Venus as one whose presence, through her affair with Adonis, cheered the mountain.

Chaucer's form looks back to OFr.

Colcos, [Lat. *Colchis, -idis* f.], an ancient district in Asia Minor at the east end of the Black (Euxine) Sea and just south of the Caucasus (*Caucasus*, above), corresponds to the lowland area Mingrelia of the Georgian S.S.R. of the Soviet Union. Celebrated in Greek mythology as the home of Medea, the land of the Golden Fleece, and the goal of Jason and his Argonauts, it is so introduced in the Legend of Hypsipyle and Medea. Mentioned in *LGW* 1580, 1591, it is said, following Guido delle Colonne (*insula*), in *LGW* 1425, 1438 incorrectly to be an *yle*, correctly (l. 1426) as *beyonde Troye, estward in the se* (Propontis and Euxine). The quest of the Golden Fleece is referred to as the *adventures of Colcos* (*LGW* 1515); in *LGW* 1593 it is a *contré*. The capital is *Jaconitos* (see below). Jason's route from his home in Thessaly (*Tessalie, LGW* 1461, and below) is reasonably plotted as crossing the Aegean Sea (*salte se, se, LGW* 1462, 1470, 1495, 1510; see further "Aegean Sea", above), with a stopover on the island of Lemnos (*Lemnoun,* l. 1463), thence by implication (see above) sailing by the Troad, through the Propontis and east out the Euxine.

Chaucer's *Colcos*, as other names in this story, derive from Guido delle Colonne's corrupt *Colcos*.

Coloigne [var. MR V, 42], Cologne (Germ. *Köln*, Du. *Keulen*, OE *Colon*, Fr. *Cologne*) on the Rhine, Germany, is mentioned in *CT* A 466 as a place to which the Wife had made a pilgrimage; the specific allusion would be to the reliquary of the Three Kings (Reliquienschrein der heiligen drei Könige), now part of the cathedral treasure. The cathedral was begun in 1248 and in the Wife's day, and indeed until long after, was only partly completed.

The name looks back to Roman *Colonia (Claudia) Agrippinensis* or *Colonia Agrippina*, founded 38 B.C. On Lat. *colonia* "farm settlement, development", see Gröhler II, 28–29. For ME and later forms see *NED s.v.* "Cologne"; Chaucer's form reflects the common OFr type *Co(u)loi(n)gne*; modern English Cologne is based on modern French; cp. similarly *Boloigne* I. For Fr. names based on Lat. *colonia* see Longnon No. 495 and Index.

[de] Columpnis for *Columnis* [Lat. ablat. plur.] "columns", Ital. *delle Colonne*, is mentioned in *HF* 1469 (3, 379) to identify Guido, author of the *Historia Destructionis Troiae* (ed. Nathaniel E. Griffin, Cambridge, Mass.: Mediaeval Academy of America, 1936). The name of this Sicilian writer, surely plural in form (vs occasional *della Colonna*), refers almost certainly to his membership in the great Roman family of Colonna (Griffin, *ed. cit.*, p. xvi); *delle Colonne* or *de Columnis* thus in effect means "(one) of the Colonna family".

The name looks back to the title of the founder of the family, Pietro (*ca* 1100 A.D.), lord of Columna (Colonna), Palestrina, and Paliano, where Columna or Colonna refers to the town of

Colonna some 15 m. SE of Rome and 4 m. NE of Frascati.
The name reflects the Latin use of *columna* to define a topo-
graphical eminence (cp. *Jubaltare*, *Pileer* and *Septe*).

cordewane, leather of Cordova [Span. *Cordoba*], Spain,
lying SW of *Gernade*, is mentioned in *CT* B² *1922 (732) to
define the leather of Sir Thopas' shoes. This Cordovan leather,
in the past often called "cordwain" (*NED s.v.*) and principally
of tanned and dressed goat-skins, was much prized in the Middle
Ages as a luxury type of shoe-leather.
    The name is based on Lat. (Iberian?) *Corduba* (Hispanica
Baetica), birthplace of Seneca and Lucan (Holder I, 1119–24).
Chaucer's and related forms look back to OFr *cordo(u)an* (OSpan.
cordovan) with which compare the modern French name of the
city, *Cordoue*; later English "cordovan" (*NED s.v.*) is a direct
borrowing from Spanish.

Corynthe, Corinth, [Lat. *Corinthus*], city and small territory
of ancient Greece just south of the Isthmus of Corinth with its
famous citadel or Acro-Corinth; the modern town of New
Corinth, founded in 1858, lies some 3 m. east of the old city.
Corinth is mentioned in *CT* C 604 as the goal of a mission by
one Stilbon, on whom see Robinson, p. 731, n. 603. Important
Corinthians, conceived of as inveterate gamblers, are *alle the
gretteste ... of that lond* (*CT* C 607).
    Chaucer's and the modern form derive from OFr.

Crete, Crete [Lat. *Creta*, *Crete*], island in the Mediterranean
SE of Greece, now Kandia. In *LGW* 1886, 1894, it defines the
kingship of the semi-legendary Minos, king of Crete in a period
well before the Trojan War; his wife Pasiphaë is mentioned as

queen of Crete in *CT* D 733; in *LGW* 2216 it is a *contré*. In *LGW* 1895 Minos is said to have a *hundred cités stronge and grete*, not necessarily all in Crete (cp. his conquest of Athens, etc. ll. 1901 ff.); in his unnamed capital is his *court* (1949) and a dungeon (*tour*, 1960) is built on to the same *wal* (1962, 1971) in which is built a privy (*foreyne*, 1962; cp. Germ. *Abort* and see further *Speculum*, IX [1934], esp. 314 ff.); this dungeon is the *prysoun* (1950, 1975, 1997, 2011) of Theseus, prince of Athens. Somehow adjoining or very near Theseus' prison is the Labyrinth (*hous*, 2012, 2141–42), constructed as a *mase* (2014), where he slays the Minator (2104, 2142, 2145), in l. 1928 named a man-eating *monstre*. This latter event is alluded to also in *CT* A 980.

Chaucer's and the modern form are based on OFr.

D

Damyssene, formally the adj. Damascene [Lat. *Damascenus*: see *NED s.v.*], of or pertaining to Damascus, chief town of the Roman province of Syria and of the modern state. In *CT* B *3197 (2007) it is used for the town of Damascus or perhaps more generally for the area round about the town (mod. Ghutah); Adam is said to have been created in the *feeld of Damyssene* "plain of Damascus", answering to a Lat. *in agro Damasceno*.

The adj. is OFr (see *NED loc. cit.*) and is based on the town-name.

Delphicus, Lat. adj. "Delphic", "of or pertaining to Delphi", is used in *TC* 1, 70 for the sake of rhyme (: *thus*) and describes Apollo. The Lat. adj. is based on the place-name Delphi (see *Delphos*, below).

Delphos, formally Lat. acc. pl. of Delphi, a site in ancient Phocis *ca* 5 m. from Cirrha (*Cirrea*, above) and the Gulf of Crisa at the foot of Mt Parnassus (*Parnaso*, below) and seat of the oracle of the Pythian (from Pytho, earlier name of Delphi) or Delphic Apollo, most famous of antiquity. The oracle is mentioned in *TC* 4, 1411, with reference to an occasion in the course of the Trojan War when Calchas visited Delphi on behalf of the Trojans, and in *CT* F 1077 where the oracle is a *temple* of the god, which Aurelius promises to visit as a barefoot pilgrim.

Depeford, Deptford [*det-ford*] (K), S.E.8, now a sizeable metropolitan borough of London, 4 to 4½ m. from Southwark (*Southwerk*) at the junction of the Ravensbourne with the Thames immediately west of *Grenewych* (*q.v.*) and now a slummy district, is mentioned in *CT* A 3906 (var. *Dartford*, MR V, 387) to define a point on the *Caunterbury Wey*, apparently between itself and Greenwich, which the pilgrims have reached at about 7.30 on the first morning after leaving Southwark (cp. *CT* A 822). That the Knight and the Miller between them should have got through with three thousand odd lines of verse in such short order is merely part of the unrealism of the whole plan and should not be pressed or in any way rationalized here or elsewhere. Muirhead *London* 455.

The name looks back to OE (*se*) *déopa ford* "(the) deep ford", presumably with reference to the Ravensbourne stream. With the unexplained intrusive -*t*- in post-Chaucerian spellings (*DEPN s.v.*) and the pronunciation cp. the Devonshire Deptfords of similar origin.

[Derteford], Dartford (K) on the Darent and 15 m. from *Southwerk*, though not mentioned by name has often been urged as the place of the first overnight stop the pilgrims would have made on the *Caunterbury Wey*, had Chaucer ever got around to dealing with the matter of overnight stops. The night here in question is usually assumed to have intervened between the end of the A Group (*CT* A 4422) and the beginning of the B Group (Man of Law's Prologue); according to *CT* B 1–6 it was 9.58 a.m. on April 18th, when Harry Bailey got the Man of Law going. See Skeat V, 132–34; Littlehales 40; Jerrold 373–77; Tatlock 481–82; Robinson 689–90, introductory note and n. 2; also *Caunterbury Wey*, above.

The name looks back to the Celtic river-name *Dærenta* and OE *ford* (DB *Tarentefort*, 1089 *Darenteford*) "ford over the Darent"; *DEPN s.v.*, *ERN* 113–14, and cp. *Dertemouthe*, below.

Dertemouthe, Dartmouth (D) on the W side of the Dart estuary, in Chaucer's day a very small settlement (Manly 523, n. 388 *ad fin.*) opposite Kingshaven, where American troops set out on June 6th, 1944, for Normandy and today the site of the Royal Naval College, is mentioned in *CT* A 389 as the possible home of the Shipman (Bowden 195–96, Muirhead *England* 172). The latter is further described as living "*fer by weste*" "way in the West" with Darmouth hazarded as where he may actually come from (see *Weste*, below).

The name reflects the Celtic river-name *Dærenta*, later *Derta* (*ERN* 114–115) and OE *múða* m. "river mouth, estuary", "the mouth of the Dart"; cp. *Derteford*, above; *PN* VIII *D* 321.

Domus Dedaly, see **Hous of Dedalus.**

Dover, Dover (K) at the mouth of the Dour, starting point of *Watlynge-Strete* (*q.v.*) to London via Canterbury and chief of the Cinque Ports, is mentioned in *CT* A 4347 to define some undetermined cooked dish, perhaps a pie of sorts, perhaps a Dover sole ("*Jakke of D.*"), at any rate much warmed over, thought by Harry Bailey to be unwholesome or unfit to eat (A 4348), and sold by Roger the Cook in his food-shop in London. Muirhead *England* 14–16.

The name looks back to Late British **Dubras* plur. "waters" with reference to the Dour river, yielding OE *Dofras* masc. plur.; the plural -*s* survives in the French name of the town *Douvres*.

Drye See, the Gobi [Chinese *Han-hai* "dry see"], great expanse of desert country in Outer Mongolia between the Tibetan massif and the Altai Mountains, is mentioned in *BD* 1028 as a point on a route including *Carre Nar* on which the Duchess of Lancaster would not have sent an admirer on an irksome or futile mission (cp. *Alysaundre, Carre Nar, Pruyce, Tartarye I, Turkye, Walakye*). For the not very likely suggestion that Chaucer's "Dry Sea" might refer to one of two areas on the Arctic coast of Russia and known to Englishmen after Chaucer's time, see Lowes, esp. pp. 27–29; the areas in question are or were called in Russian *sukhoe more* "dry sea" and are respectively at the mouth of the Petschora and at the east mouth of the Dviná by Archangel.

This name, reaching Chaucer through unknown channels and perhaps quite familiar to travellers of the time, is merely a translation of the Chinese *Han-hai* "dry sea", alternative designation for the Gobi, commonly called *Sha-mo* "sand desert" (see Lowes, esp. p. 17, for the term "Sandy Sea"). Also see Lowes *passim* for references to these designations in various contemporary and later writings. The modern name is Mongolian *gobi* "desert". For the practice, unusual in Chaucer, of translating foreign place-names, cp. *Newe Toun*.

Duche, of or pertaining to Germany (High or Low), German (High or Low), is used in *HF* 1234 (3, 144) to define the language (*Duche tonge*) of pipers (MHG *pfifers*, MLG *pîpaere*), musicians who might play any of several wood-wind instruments and who were often able and expected to double on the strings. On the use of *Duche*, later Dutch, to embrace both High and Low German speech (High and Low Dutch of the fairly recent past) see *NED s.v.* B1 and cp. Du. *duitsch* "German" (not Dutch!), Germ. *deutsch*. Here there would be no very obvious way of knowing whether Chaucer had in mind "pipers" whose speech was Low or High German for they were ubiquitous, and it is scarcely conceivable that the matter would have been of concern to him.

Duche and its cognates look back to an Old-Germanic **peu-disk-* (cp. Lat. *Teutones*), signifying "national, popular"; see *NED s.v.* "Dutch", headnote.

Dunmowe, Dunmow Priory, Little Dunmow (Ess), is mentioned in *CT* D 218 by the Wife in reference to the local custom by which in her time and intermittently ever since a flitch of bacon (D 217) might at a ceremony or "trial by jury" (modern) be claimed by any married couple who had not quarrelled or regretted their marriage in a year and a day. In Chaucer's day the oath was taken before the prior of Dunmow Priory (now a ruin) at Little Dunmow, 2½ m. SE of the present town (photos of Priory in Steer, Pl II–IV). For a full-length treatment of this, see Francis W. Steer, *The History of the Dunmow Flitch Ceremony* (Essex Record Office Publ. 13), Chelmsford (Essex County

Council) 1951, with many illustrations; Manly 578, n. 218; see additionally Chester L. Shaver, 'A Mediaeval French Analogue to the Dunmow Flitch', *Modern Language Notes*, L (1935), 322–25, with much documentation on the custom in England, and a sprightly contemporary account by Atcheson L. Hench, 'Dunmow Bacon, 1949', *College English*, XI (1950), 350, expanded in 'The Dunmow Flitch Trials', *Southern Folklore Quarterly*, XVI (1952), 128–31. The most recent Dunmow Flitch Trial was held in June 1960 and it is the local intention to hold them henceforth at five-year intervals; this has been also made familiar through the Dunmow Flitch Bacon Company Ltd., whose vans are often to be seen in the London area and elsewhere. Muirhead *England* 587.

The name looks back to OE *dún* "hill" and **máwe* "mowed place, meadow"; *PN*, XII *Ess*, 474–75.

E

Ebrayk, see **(H)ebrayk,** below.

Egipcien, A. adj. Egyptian [Lat. *Aegyptianus*, Fr. *égyptien*] in *CT* B 500 qualifies the semi-legendary St Mary of Egypt.

B. sb. an Egyptian, mentioned in *CT* B *3528 (2338) in a catalog of peoples not brave enough to face Queen Zenobia of Palmyra (*Palymerie*, below) in battle.

Egipt[e], Egypt [Lat. *Aegyptus*], viewed as forming a part of Asia until the time of Ptolemy I (*regn.* 311 ?–285 B.C.), who declared the isthmus of Suez and the Red Sea to be the boundary between the continents of Africa and Asia; since then Egypt has been viewed as forming the NE extremity of Africa. In Chaucer Egypt is mentioned in two main connections.

A. As the site of the Biblical story of Joseph, son of Jacob and Rachel: so in *BD* 280–81 it defines Joseph and in *CT* B *4323 (3133) an unidentified Hykson, king of Egypt of the fifteenth-sixteenth dynasties, Pharaoh and Joseph's friend and patron; both passages have to do with Joseph as an interpreter of dreams (cp. *Gen.* xli, 25 ff.).

B. In connection with the romantic story of Antony and Cleopatra (d. 30 B.C.), daughter of Ptolemy Auletes (d. 51 B.C.): so in *LGW* 581 *Egipt* is said to have passed under the rule of Cleopatra (*regn.* 52–49, 48–30 B.C.) after the death of her father, and in *LGW* 674 it is a land rich in precious stones used by Cleopatra to adorn her shrine. In *CT* B 500, 501 mention is made of a *cave* and the *desert*.

In *BD* 1207 the *ten woundes of Egipte* is a rendering of sorts, though wrong, of the so-called *dies Aegyptiaci* "Egyptian (i.e., unlucky) Days" of mediaeval calenders.

Chaucer's and the modern form is from OFr (mod. *Egypte*).

[**Elea,** also called **Velia**] in the ancient South Italian district of Lucania, now Castelammare della Bruca at the mouth of the Alento (prov. Campania), was the birthplace of the philosopher Zeno "of Elea" and founder of the Eleatic school; the name is implied in the phrase "*in the studies and scoles of Eleaticis and Achademycis in Grece*" (*Bo* 1, pr. 1, l. 74 (30–35).

Elicon[e], formally Mt Helicon of antiquity (mod. Zagora) a mountain range in Boeotia some 25 m. SE of Mt Parnassus (*Parnaso,* below) and Delphi (*Delphos,* above), celebrated in antiquity as an abode of the Muses with a temple and grove sacred to them. It is mentioned in *HF* 521–22, (2, 13–14) correctly as the abode of the Muses while the *clere welle* "clear spring" might be taken to refer to the famous fountains of

Aganippe and Hippocrene (but see below); in *TC* 3, 1809–10 it is wrongly located on or near Parnassus. In *Anel* 17 it is on Parnassus and near Cirrha-Crisa. From a practical point of view Helicon as an abode of the Muses has been confused with Castalia or the Castalian Spring (mod. Aio Janni) flowing out of the gorge framed by the cliffs named Phaedriadae, sacred to Apollo and the Muses; on this confusion already found in post-classical authors see Robinson, p. 782, col. 1, n. 520 ff.

Elisos, as if a distortion of the Lat. m. acc. pl. *Elysios* of *Elysii* "the Elysian Fields" (in full *Elysii Campi*), Elysium, mythological abode of good persons and heroes exempt from death. It is mentioned in *TC* 4, 790, as a final happy refuge of Troilus and Criseyde, and in l. 789 is defined a*s the feld of pité*, on which special and peculiar definition, see Robinson. p. 830, n. 788 ff.

Eltham, Eltham [K], S.E.9, suburban village in the metro-politan borough of Woolwich 7¾ m. SE of London Bridge Station, is mentioned in *LGW* Prol. F 497 (omitted in G) with reference to Eltham Palace (now some ruins), a favorite royal residence from Henry III (1270) to James I (1612), as a place alternate to *Sheene* (*q.v.*), where Chaucer is to deliver the completed *Legend of Good Women* to Richard II's first queen, Anne of Bohemia (died June 7th, 1394). Muirhead *London* 492–93.

The name is of disputed origin but may look back to OE *Eltan-hám "*Elta's manor"; *DEPN s.v.*

Emele [var. MR VI, 248] as an infix in *To-Emele-ward*, Emilia (Lat. *Aemilia*), division of N. Italy lying S of the *Poo*, is mentioned in *CT* E 51 along with *Ferrare* and *Venyse* to plot the course of the river; Chaucer is here drawing directly on Petrarch (B & D 296, 8).

The name is based on that of the Rom. province named after Aemilius Lepidus, builder of the *Via Aemilia*. Chaucer's *Emele* vs an expected *Emelye* may have been adapted arbitrarily *metri causa* or may answer to some OFr variant form; cp. his *Arabe*, alternate to *Arabye*.

Engelond, England, is mentioned in *CT* A 14 (its shires are referred to in A 15), 580, 2113, C 912, D 1322, 1340, G 1356; in B 1130 it defines Alla's kingdom, elsewhere *Northumberland*, *q.v.;* in F 810 it is further defined as a country *"that cleped was eek Briteyne"* (in opposition to Brittany, France; see *Britaygne*, above).

The name looks back to late OE *Engla-land* "England" "land of the Angles" (OE *Engle*), which displaced earlier *Engla-cynn* "race of the Angles". It is not unlikely that the ethnic name *Engle* was originally pronounced with a palatal *ng* and that the pronunciation *ng* was due to, or influenced by, ON **Engla-land*, mod. Icel. *England*. Cp. *Scotland*, below.

English, sb. the English language, is used in *CT* A 22, 265, 1459, B 49, F 37, G 87; *BD* 898; *TC* 5, 1794; *LGW* 1382; *Anel* 9, *Venus* 80.

The word looks back to OE *Englisc*, later probably under Scandinavian influence *Englisc*; see *Engelond*, above.

Ennopye, Oenopia [Lat. *Oenopia*], older name of Aegina, island in the Saronic Gulf, now Gulf of Egina, between Attica and the Peloponnesus (now Morea), is mentioned in *LGW* 2155 as a *contré* and refuge of Theseus, Ariadne, Phaedra, and Theseus' friendly jailer.

[ad] Ephesios, Lat. acc. pl., Ephesians [Lat. *Ephesii*], natives of Ephesus, commercial town in Ionia (Asia Minor), whose ruins are near the modern village of Ayasuluk (prov. of Izmir), Turkey, are mentioned in *CT* I 748 with reference to St Paul's Epistle to the Ephesians (*Ephes.* v, 5).

Ermyn, adj. sb., an Armenian, native inhabitant of Armenia, is mentioned in *CT* B*3528 (2338) as one of a number of nationals who dared not oppose Queen Zenobia of Palmyra (*Palmyrie*, below) in battle.

Chaucer's form is OFr vs mod. *arménien* and is based on the regional name *Ermony*, below.

Ermony, Armenia [Lat. *Armenia*], classical name of Hebrew Ararat, a country extending between the shore of Lake Van, the upper Euphrates (*Eufrates*, below), and Media (*Mede*, below), is used, probably fancifully, in *Anel* 72 to define the queenship of Anelida, who resides in a *toun* there.

Chaucer's form is based on OFr *Ermenie* (mod. Arménie) which in OFr is also used for the land of the Saracens. The native name was *Biana*, mod. Armenian *Van*.

Essex, Essex, is mentioned in *CT* D 218 [var. MR V, 25] as the county in which *Dunmowe* is situated.

The name looks back to OE *Éast-Seaxe* "East Saxons" or, better, to such phrases as *on Éast-Seaxum* "among the East-Saxons", i.e., "in Essex"; *PN* XII *Ess* 1.

Est-see is mentioned in *TC* 5, 1109 implicitly as the first body of water to be warmed by the rising sun and would appear to be thought of as east of Troy. In this respect the passage may be compared with the ninth or early tenth-century Germano-Latin *Waltharius*, l. 1189: *Taprobane clarum videt insula solem* (Taprobane [i.e., Ceylon] is already seeing the bright sun), this observation being made as the first rays of dawn are striking Mt Olympus. Hence, *Est-see* would seem quite possibly, indeed not unlikely and/or despite Guido, to refer to the Indian Ocean rather than some vague, actually non-existent, body of water lying east of Troy, as is urged by Robert A. Pratt, 'A Geographical Problem in *Troilus and Criseyde*', *Mod. Lang. Notes*, LXI (1946), 541–43.

Ethiopeen, adj.-sb. Ethiopian, inhabitant of Ethiopia [Lat. *Aethiopia*], with the common implication of blackamoor or African negro, is used in *CT* I, 344 (345–50) to describe the color of St Jerome's skin after exposure to the desert sun. In the OFr romances *Ethiope* (mod. *Ethiopie*) was viewed as a Saracen country and may have been so viewed by Chaucer.

Chaucer's form is OFr *Ethiopien, -en*; for many instances see *MED s.v.*

Ethna, Etna, the largest volcano of Europe [Lat. *Aetna*], rising on the east coast of Sicily. In *Bo* 2, m. 5, l. 35 (480–85) and pr. 6, l. 8 (485–90) it is the *mountaigne of Ethna*; in the first instance its *fyer* is said to burn as does human greed, in the second its *flaumbe*, when the latter surges up, does more damage than wicked men do. In *CT* E 2230 the volcano is mentioned in connection with the rape of Proserpina by the underworld god Pluto.

Chaucer's form is Latin with a decorative, silent *h*.

Eufrates, the great Mesopotamian river Euphrates [Lat. *Euphrates*, Turk. *Frat su*] whose main stream (north branch) rises in Dumlu Dagh (ancient Taurus range) NNW of Erzerum (ancient Theodosiopolis). In *Bo* 5, m. 1, ll. 1, 7 (1640–45, 1645–50), it is said wrongly to rise from a common source with the Tigris (*Tygris*, below); it is then said to separate from the Tigris (ll. 7–8), later and correctly said to unite with the latter in a mighty stream (ll. 8–9, 15); the juncture of the two rivers is just below Korna.

Eurippe, Lat. *Euripus*, channel between Boeotia (and Attica) and the island of Euboea, at whose narrowest point, opposite Chalcis on Euboea, it is only 120 ft wide; the channel is remarkable for extraordinary changes of current. The strait is mentioned twice in *Bo* 2, m. 1, ll. 3–4 (290–95), where it is described as *boylynge*, while the immediately following gloss, where it is an *arm of the see*, speaks of the characteristic changes in the course of the current.

Chaucer's form is OFr.

Europe, Europe [Lat. *Europa*] is mentioned in *HF* 1339 (3, 249) and *CT* B 161 with reference to the whole European continent.

The name, first recorded in the Homeric *Hymn to Apollo* and first used with the modern distinction between Europe and Asia by Aeschylus, was probably transmitted to the Greeks from the east, perhaps from Assyria.

Chaucer's and the mod. form are French.

[Euxine or **Black Sea]** [Lat. *Euxinus Pontus*] is referred to as *the se* in *LGW* 1426 at the east end of which (*estward in* *the se*) is the district of Colchis (*Colcos*, above). The outspoken modern name describes its fogs and inhospitable character.

F

Fay[e]rye, essentially the land or home of fays (OFr *fae*, mod. *fée*) or supernatural beings possessed of miraculous powers, is used to designate:

A. The underworld of antiquity of which Pluto is king in *CT* E 2227, 2234, and Proserpina *a queene* (E 2316).

B. In a less definite sense in *CT* F 96 as the or an underworld from which Sir Gawain might conceivably return to earth.

C. An enchanted land or *contré*, yet on this earth, in which Sir Thopas finds himself in *CT* B *1992 (802). In *CT* B *1991 (801) it is a secret place (*pryvé woon*), ruled by an elfin queen (*elf-queene*, B *1989 [799]), in B *2004 (814) called the *queene of F.*

Chaucer's form is OFr *fae(i)rie*, mod. *féerie*; see *NED* under "*faerie*", "*fairy*, A.1".

Femenye, as if Lat. **Feminia* "land of women," is used specifically of the legendary land of the Amazons, female warriors whose queen Hippolyta, wedded to Theseus, and her sister Emelye (in ancient legend Antiope) are brought back by Theseus to Athens. Hippolyta's realm (*regne of Femenye*) is mentioned in *CT* A 866, 877 where it is equated with Scythia (*Scithia*, below); the people are *Amazones* (*CT* A 880).

In the OFr romances *Femenie* is thought of as a land beyond the Red Sea, with Saracen associations, and Chaucer may have thought of it thus, if indeed he gave the matter any thought at all. In antiquity the land of the Amazons was thought of as bordering the river Thermodon, now the Terme çayı, flowing into the Black Sea (Pontus Euxinus), just east of the Turkish city of Tçarçembe.

The geography here could scarcely be more confused. Chaucer's form is OFr.

Ferrare [var. MR VI, 248] in Chaucer probably refers to what is now more or less the province of Ferrara rather than to the Emilian city itself which is situated not on the *Poo* proper but on the branch known as the Po di Vomano; it is mentioned in *CT* E 51 along with *Emele* and *Venyse* to plot the course of the river.

This place-name seems to be based on the stem of Ital. *ferro* "iron" *ferraria, ferriera* "smithy, iron-works" (Dante Olivieri, *Dizionario etimologico italiano* (Milan, 1953), *s.v.* "ferro", but the settlement itself is of uncertain, post-Roman origin and presumably mediaeval (*EI* XV, 41); it is not to be identified with any known Roman settlement such as *Forum Alieni* of Gallia Transpadana as given in some dictionaries. Chaucer has here substituted *Ferrare* for Petrarch's *Flaminia* (B & D 296, 8), the latter used by Petrarch in a learned sort of way (cp. *Venyse*) with reference to the Roman judicial district *Flaminia*, set up in the second century A.D. and corresponding to the former territory of the Senones.

Fynstere [Cape of] [var. MR V, 6], Cape Finistere (Span. *Capo de Finisterre*), north-western headland of the region of Galicia (now prov. Coruña), Spain, is mentioned in *CT* A 408 as the southern terminus of a stretch of European coast, of which *Gootland* is the northern, very familiar to the Shipman. This headland, some 40 m. due W of *Seint-Jame*, must also

have been a familiar and cheering sight to many English pilgrims
of Chaucer's day who proceeded to the shrine of Santiago by
sea and who were on the point of rounding the cape to enter,
say, the port of Padrón. Finistère in Brittany (Gröher II, 140),
westernmost department of France with its capital Quimper,
cannot be thought of here.

The name is a learned and obvious construction, based on
Med. Lat. *finis terrae*, with which compare *Land's End* in
Cornwall and the French department name.

Flaundres, Flanders [Fr. *Flandre*, Du. *Vlaanderen*], in
Chaucer's day a countship and essentially that part of present-
day Belgium (West Flanders) bounded on the E by the Schelde
and including the towns of *Brugges*, *Gaunt*, *Ypres*, and *Popering*;
it was bounded on the S by the county of *Artoys*. In *CT* A 86
it is one of the areas along with *Artoys* and *Pycardie* where the
Squire had fought. In B² *1908–09 it is the homeland of Sir
Thopas, a *fer contree* and *al biyonde the See* (i.e., North Sea),
in *1912 it is the *contree* of which Sir Thopas' father is *lord*,
as if doubling for Louis II de Mâle, Count of Flanders, 1346–
1382! In C 463 it is the homeland of the three dissolute crimi-
nals of the Pardoner's Tale, and in B² *1389 (199), *1429 (239),
*1490 (300) it is the goal, specifically *Brugges*, of a business
trip made by a French banker from *Seint-Denys*.

The name is of uncertain origin; for speculations see *NGT*
III, 164–65 and *OGN* 85–86. Chaucer's form with *au* (so in
Alysaundre, *Fraunce*, *Gaunt*) reflects a normanization of OFr
plur. *Les Flandres*.

Flaundryssh [var. MR V, 23], adj. rare and obs. (*NED*
and *MED s.v.* "Flandrish"), of or pertaining to Flanders, Fle-

mish, made in Flanders or in the Flemish style, is used in *CT*
A 272 to define the Merchant's beaver (*NED s.v.* 2b, 3) or
hat made of beaver's fur (*bever-hat*, Du. *beverin hoed*, Fr.
chapeau de castor), later often called a "caster" or "castor"
(*NED s.v.*, sb.,[1] 3). It would seem that there are very few documents on the Flemish hatters' trade since the latter played no
great part (vs the textile industry) in the economy of the cities
of medieval Flanders. There is some brief discussion of the
hatters' guild in Bruges in Jean Gailliard, *De Ambachten en
Neringen van Brugge*, etc. (Bruges, 1851), Pt ii, pp. 183–84, also
in Victor Gaillard, 'Etudes sur le commerce de la Flandre au
Moyen Age', *Annales de la Société d'Emulation pour l'Etude
de l'Histoire et des Antiquités de la Flandre*, XII (2e sér., VIII)
(Bruges, 1850), 118(c), where reference is to Lappenberg's
Urkundliche Geschichte der deutschen Hanse, also p. 126 under
"Castor (peaux de)". For the general tenor of the above state-
ment and the two references given I am grateful to Professor
René Derolez of the University of Gent. On the sale of this
fashionable headgear in Chaucer's London see Manly 514, n.
270 ff.

The adj. *Flaundryssh* is based on *Flaundres* plus the English
suffix *-ish*. If the samples in the *NED* and *MED* are statistically
valid, this was in Chaucer's day, as later, a relatively rare or
unusual alternate to the adj. "Flemish" of identical meaning.

Flegetoun, the Phlegethon, mythological river of the Greek
underworld, flowing with fire instead of water. In *TC* 3, 1600,
it is the *fiery flood of helle*, mentioned as a place from which
Troilus' soul has been saved.

Chaucer's form is OFr.

Fra[u]nce, in Chaucer's day a general term for most of the area now identified with France, is mentioned in various connections. As a whole it is referred to in *RR* 495 (*Roman de la Rose* 483: *tot le reiaume de France*) as *all the rewme of France* and in the same words in *CT* B² *1306 (116); the melody of the roundel at the end of *PF* is said to have been *imaked ... in Fraunce* (*PF* 677); in *Ven* 82 Otes or Oton de Granson is said to be the flower of the poets of France. In *CT* F 1118 *Orliens* is said to be in France. Finally, in *CT* B² *1341 (151) *Fraunce* identifies St Denis, patron saint of the country, and in B² *1384 (194) the traitor Ganelon of the *Chanson de Roland*.

For special parts of France, see *Artoys, Britai(g)ne* II, *Burgoyne, Loreyne, Pycardie,* also the cities of *Arras, Boloigne* I, *Burdeux, Kayrrud, Orliens, Parys, Pedmark, Reynes, (The) Rochele, Seint-Denys,* and *Valence,* the rivers *Oyse* and *Sayne,* and the arm of the sea *Gerounde.*

The name *Fraunce* (Med. Lat. *Francia*), like *Burgoyne* and *Loreyne,* is Germanic and is based on the tribal name of the Rhineland Franks, first applied to an area extending from about Soissons (dép. Aisne) to the Loire; see Gröhler II, 6; *Reallexikon* II, 83, col. 1, § 6. Chaucer's *au* (so in *Alysaundre, Flaundres, Gaunt*) reflects a normanization of OFr *France.*

Frenssh, I. adj. of or pertaining to France, French, is used in *CT* I 248 to indicate the national origin of a contemporary song "*J'ay tout perdu mon temps et mon labour*"; see Robinson 768, n. 248.

II. adj., sb., French, the French language, is referred to in *CT* A 124 for whatever sort of French the Prioress spoke as contrasted to the Parisian French of A 126; cp. *Stratford-atte-Bowe.*

Frenssh looks back to OE *Frenčisc*, based with *i*-mutation on the element *Franc-* in OE *Francland*, Lat. *Francia*, or the like.

Frise, Friesland, also Frisia (Du. *Vriesland*, Fris. *Fryslân*, Fr. *Frise*), coupled with *Rome*, is mentioned in *RR* 1093 (not in *Roman de la Rose* 1076) to suggest—somewhat oddly—a source of great amounts of gold more precious than the jewelled chape in a girdle worn by Richesse. Chaucer surely picked this name at random (: *noble wise*). *Frise* is mentioned in *Buk* 23 as a region unpleasant, even perilous, to be taken prisoner in, yet better perhaps than to be trapped into marriage! Chaucer may have had in mind a rather shortlived and abortive expedition by Count Albrecht of Holland, supported by French and Bavarian knights and English archers, against West Lauwers Friesland in August–September 1396; see Skeat I, 558–59, n.

Chaucer's form is French. The name is of uncertain origin but appears as *Frisii* "Frisians" as early as Pliny and Tacitus; see *Reallexikon* II, 100–01, § 7.

I. **Frygius,** Lat. adj. [Lat. *Phrygius*], Phrygian, pertaining to the ancient country of Phrygia in central and northern Asia Minor, of varying boundaries but at times including the Troad. In *BD* 1070 it is used to define Dares, supporter of Troy in the war against the Greeks and suppositious author of the epitomized account of the war from the Trojan point of view, *de Excidio Troiae Historia.*

II. **Frigius,** [Lat. *Phrygius*], a Phrygian, native of ancient Phrygia, a country of varying destinies and boundaries in NW Asia Minor, is used in *BD* 1064 to define one Dares, supposititiosu author of a tract *de Excidio Troiae Historia* (A.D. 400–600?), presenting in digest form the Trojan story from the Trojan point of view; Dares is also mentioned, though without further definition, in *HF* 1467 (3, 377) and *TC* 1, 146, 5, 1771.

G

Galgopheye, a distortion of Gargaphia [Lat. *Gargaphia, -phie*], valley in Boeotia sacred to Diana, with a fountain of the same name where Actaeon was turned into a stag and was torn to pieces by hounds. In *CT* A 2626 it is mentioned as *vale* inhabited by fierce mother-tigresses.

Galice, Galicia, prov. Coruña, Spain, formerly an independent kingdom but in Chaucer's day a part of the kingdom of Castile, is mentioned in *CT* A 466 to locate *Seint-Jame*.

The name (Rom. *Call[a]ecia, Gallaicia*) is based on the Iberian tribal name *Call(a)eci, Gallaici* (Holder I, 701, 1638); Chaucer's form is French. (It may be noted that the Spanish name has nothing to do with Galicia, now partly in Poland, partly in the Ukraine [Russ. *Galich, Galitsiya*, Ukrain. *Halicz*, Germ. *Galizien*], mediaeval Polish principality, based on the name *Galich*, once an important town, now an insignificant village.)

Galilee, Galilee [Lat. *Galilaea*], in Roman times the northernmost province of Palestine, is used in *CT* D 11 to identify Cana (*Cane*, above). The Sea of Galilee is referred to as *the see* in *CT* A 698 with reference to *Matth.* xiv, 29.

Gatesden, (Great) Gaddesden (Herts) on the Gade, presumed home of the physician "*John of G.*" (1280?–1361) or of his family, is mentioned in *CT* A 434 (var. MR V, 39) in a list of medical men, Greek, Arabian, and English; *DNB* VII, 787–88.

The name probably looks back to an OE personal name *Gǽte* < *gát* f. "goat" and *denu* f. "dene, valley". The river name Gade is a back-formation; see *DEPN s.v.* "Gaddesden" and *ERN* 168.

Gaunt, Ghent [Du. *Gent*, Fr. *Gand*], capital of East Flanders, Belgium, at the junction of the Lys (Du. *Leie*) and the Schelde or Schelt (Fr. *Escaut*), was in Chaucer's day at the height of its prosperity as the center of a great textile industry in connection with which it is mentioned in *RR* 574 (*Roman de la Rose* 564: *Ganz*) and *CT* A 448.

The name is first recorded as Med. Lat. *Gandavum* (Holder I, 1981), apparently based on a stem *Gand-* of unknown origin and meaning; see *NGF* III, 47; *OGN* 127–28; Förster *Themse* 312–13, n. 1, 442, n. 1. Chaucer's form, still familiar in the name of the great Duke of Lancaster, John of Gaunt, reflects with its *au* (so *Alysaundre*, *Flaundres*, *Fraunce*) a normanized form of OFr *Gant* without *i*-mutation vs OE *Gend* and the modern Dutch and English forms with *i*-mutation.

Gawle, formally Gaul [Lat. *Gallia*], in antiquity an area answering in part to modern France. In *CT* F 1411 the *folk of Gawle* refers not to the ancient Gauls of Caesar but to an eastward migrating splinter group, more properly referred to as Galatians (Lat. *Galatae*) or Gallograeci, which invaded Asia Minor in 278–277 B.C. and in 276 sacked the Carian city of Miletus (*Melesie*, below).

The form is OFr, mod. *Gaule*.

Gazan, Gaza [Lat. *Gaza,* mod. Arabic Ghazzeh], one of the chief towns of the Philistines in Palestine (mod. Syria), is mentioned in *CT* B *3237 (2047) in connection with the story of Sampson (*Judges* 13–16); it is a *cité* (B *3238 [2048]) or *toun* (B *3239 [2049]) with *gates* (B *3239 [2049]) and a nearby *hill* (B *3241 [2051]). The great stone *temple* is mentioned in B *3272 (2082), *3275 (2085), 3279 (2089) with pillars (*pilers,* B *3274 [2084]), destroyed by Sampson; Sampson's prison is in a *cave* (B *3263 [2073]) and he is set to work at a hand-mill (*queerne,* B *3264 [2074]).

The form *Gazan* is perhaps based on Lat. acc. *Gazam* of *Judges* xvi, 1, and despite the var. *Gaza* would seem to be Chaucer's form.

Gernade [Var. MR V, 6], Granada on the Genil or Jenil (Romano-Iberian *Singilis,* later Arab. *Shinīl,* Holder II, 572 "Singilia"), in Chaucer's day capital of the independent Moorish kingdom of Granada, now chief town of the maritime province of Granada, S. Spain, is mentioned in *CT* A 56 as a place at the siege of which the Knight had been; see Robinson 652, col. 1 "The Knight".

The origin of the name is disputed but perhaps looks back to Arab. *Qarnatta* (*al-Yahud*) "hill (of the Jews)"; more doubtful would be a derivation from the common noun *granada* "pomegranate" which appears on the city's coat of arms (but see *E Isl* II,[2] 175–77) and may represent a popular etymology, comparable to the later identification of the Swiss capital *Bern(e)* (from Italian *Verona*) with "bear"; on this latter see *MS* VII, 91–92 "Berne".

Gerounde [var. MR VI, 629] refers in *CT* F 1222 to the Gironde, estuary or arm of the sea some 45 m. long beginning

at the juncture of the Garonne and the Dordogne and is said
to be the southern limit, of which the *Sayne* is the northern, of
a stretch of French coast from which a scholar of *Orliens* in
the Franklin's Tale is to remove all rocks and reefs. Cp. Elias
Lönnrot's *Kalevala*, Poem 40, ll. 41–60.

The name is perhaps etymologically to be associated with
the brook-name Gironde (dép. Hautes-Alpes); see Holder I,
2014 "*Gerontona".

Gysen, a distortion, long antedating Chaucer, of Gyndes
[Lat. *Gyndes*, acc. *-en*], now Diala or Kerkah(?), tributary of
the Tigris (*Tigrys*, below), which joins the latter below the site
of Baghdad, is mentioned in *CT* D 2080 in connection with
Cyrus' futile and angry gesture of "destroying" the river by
diverting it into 360 rivulets and thus drying it up, a story
derived from Lucius Annaeus Seneca's dialogue, *De Ira* III,
21, § 3.

The Gyndes river (acc. *Gynden*) appears wrongly as *Gygem*
or *Gigen* in all manuscripts of Seneca's work, as if somehow
associated with King Gyges of Lydia, and was first put right
by Erasmus. Chaucer's copy of Seneca all but surely had *Gysen*
for *Gynden* of the modern standard editions of Seneca.

Gootland [var. *Gut-*, *Guth-land*, MR V, 36], most likely
Gottland or Gotland (official Swed. *Gotland*, OSwed. *Gotland*,
Old Gutnish *Gutaland*), island in the Baltic and a prov. of
Sweden, is mentioned in *CT* A 408 as the northern terminus,
of which *Fynystere* was the southern, of a stretch of European
coast familiar to the Shipman. Identification of Chaucer's
name with this island with its once great trading center of Visby
seems very likely despite one phonetic imperfection. The weak

link here is the long *o* (*oo* of most Mss.) as pointed out by Kemp
Malone, "King Alfred's 'Geats'", *Modern Language Review*,
XX (1925), 6, who urged identification with the Danish peninsula of Jutland (Dan. Jylland); as he in effect says, a cape-to-
cape delimitation would be very neat. But it is hard to feel
sure about the curious Alfredian *Gotland*, apparently Jutland,
vs his *Gotland* "Gotland", while the six-century time-gap between Alfred and Chaucer (with no intervening support) is
very great.

The first element of Gotland is related by vowel gradation
to the name of the Goths and to that of the early inhabitants
of Swedish (Öster)götland (ON *Gautar*, OE ȝéatas). The origin
of the name of the Jutes and of Jutland (ON *Jótaland*, OSwed.
Jútaland) is obscure; *Reallexikon* II, 623, "Jüten".

Gothes, Ostrogoths (Lat. *Goti, Gothi*) is mentioned in *Bo* 1,
pr. 4, l. 82 (115–20) to define the kingship of Theodoric, sole
ruler of Italy 493–526 A.D.

Chaucer's form with an ornamental and doubtless silent *h*
(cp. Shakespeare's pun of "goats" and "Gotes" in *AYL* III,
iii, 9), derives from French; the modern pronunciation with a
false "th" is late (see *NED s.v.* "Goth").

Greece, ancient Greece, referred to in general in *TC* 1,
609; *LGW* 2271; *CT* A 962 (perhaps as opposed to Thebes)
F. 1444. It is mentioned as distinct from Thebes in *Anel.* 53
(cp. *CT* A 962), as the country of Penelope in *BD* 1081, as the
home-land of Danaus (wrongly for Aegyptus) in *LGW* 2562,
as the land of the Academia or Academe of Plato near Athens
and of the Eleatic School of Zeno in Elea (Lat. *Velia*, mod.
Castlleamare della Bruca, prov. Campania, Italy), this latter

locality bringing the definition of Greece to include Magna
Graecia (*Bo* 1, pr. 1, l. 74 [30–35]). In *LGW* 1886 *Grece* appears
as a variant for *Crete*, apparently wrongly. *Grece the contré* of
CT B *3847 (2657) embraces Macedonia (*Macedoyne*, below),
kingdom of Alexander the Great.

In *TC* 5, 924, Diomedes would rather serve Criseyde than
be king of twelve Greece's (*Greces twelve*), and the *folk of Grece*
of TC 5, 123, is equivalent to *Grekes* (cp. 1. *Greek*, below),
while the *See of Greece* of *CT* B 464 is one of Chaucer's terms
for the Mediterranean, *q.v.*, below.

Chaucer's and the modern form look back to OFr *Grece*.

I. Gre[e]k, sb.

1. A native of ancient Greece and, unless otherwise noted, a
Greek opponent of the Trojans in the siege of Troy (*Troie*,
below): *BD* 1167, *LGW* Prol. G 275; *CT* D 744 (ancient Greeks
in general); *CT* A 2899, 2951, 2959, 2969 (Athenians); *HF* 1479
(3, 389); *TC* 1, 57, 73, 135, 137, 148, 477, 483, 553, 578, 802,
1046, 1075; 2, 154, 194, 198, 511; 3, 544; 4, 30, 34, 57 (var.),
65, 82, 176, 332, 1348, 1363 (var.), 1411 (var.), 1466, 1473,
1486; 5, 118, 125, 141, 688, 861, 893, 918, 960, 967, 1000, 1465,
1581, 1756, 1801; *LGW* 931.

2. Used attributively to describe a person as of Greek origin:
BD 667; *HF* 152; *CT* B *4418 (3228).

Chaucer's and the modern form may well look back to OE
Grécas "Greeks" vs the more normal OE *Crécas*.

II. Gre[e]k, Gre[e]c, adj.

1. Pertaining to a native of ancient Greece as in *TC* 2, 1112;
Astr. Prol. l. 35.

2. Used absolutely for the language of ancient Greece, Greek

studies in general, in *Bo* 2, pr. 2, l. 81, (315–20); 3, pr. 12, l. 212 (1110–15); 4, pr. 6, l. 283 (1515–20); 5, pr. 2, l. 53 (1660–65); *Astr.* Prol. l. 36 (5–11), Pt. 1, § 21, l. 60 (100–08).

Chaucer's and the modern form may look back to the substantive (1. *Greek*, above), also influenced by OFr *grec*.

Grekissh, -yssh, Grykkyssh, adj. 1. Of or pertaining to ancient Greece or the Greeks, Greeks, Grecian, Greekish (archaic): *Bo* 4, m. 7, l. 10 (1595–1600). 2. With reference to letters (pi, tau) of the Greek alphabet: *Bo* 1, pr. 1, ll. 32, 34–35 (15–20, 20–25).

This now archaic adj. looks back to OE *grécisc* "Greek" vs the more normal OE *crécisc*. Cp. *Troiannysh*, below.

Grenewych, Greenwich (K), S.E.10, now a metropolitan borough of London, 5 m. S of London Bridge, until recently especially famous as the site of the Royal Observatory, is mentioned in *CT* A 3907 in close conjunction with *Depeford* as a point on the *Caunterbury Wey* perhaps between which and Deptford the pilgrims have reached at the beginning of the Reeve's Tale. Muirhead *London* 455.

The name looks back to OE *gréne* "green" and *wíć* "farm, farmstead".

H

Hayles, Hailes Abbey (Gl), founded in 1246, now a ruin 2 m. NE of Winchcombe (Gl) on the Isbourne and 6 m. NE of Cheltenham, is mentioned in *CT* C 656 by one of the three revellers in the Pardoner's Tale in connection with its relic of the Holy Blood. See Skeat's note V, 284–85; Manly 620–21; Muirhead *England* 297.

The name is derived from Hail brook which runs past the site and into the Isbourne and is of uncertain origin; see *ERN* 188–89.

[H]ebrayk, adj. Hebrew [Lat. *Hebraicus*], Israelitish, Jewish. In *CT* B 489 it defines *peple* and refers to the Hebrews of the time of Moses (*Exod.* xiv, 21–31); in *HF* 1433 (3, 343) it defines the Jewish historian Flavius Josephus (A.D. 37–*ca* 95); in *CT* B *1750 (560) the *Hebrayk peple*, apostrophized by Satan, are residents of the Jewish quarter (*Jewerie*, below) in an unidentified town in Asia Minor. The language (*Ebrew*) is mentioned in *Astr.* Prol. 37 (5–11). See further *Jew*, below.

Chaucer's form is adapted from the Lat. *Hebraicus*.

Helle [OE *hell*], Hades, Orcus, the pagan underworld of shades, is in Chaucer ruled by Pluto who is also king of fairyland (*CT* E 2227: *Fayerye*). In most instances *Helle* refers to the Christian hell, even in such works pretending to a pagan background as *TC*. It is mentioned in *CT* A 1200, B *3292 (2102); *BD* 589; *HF* 72, 441, 445, 1510 (3, 420); *PF* 32; *Bo* 3, m. 12, ll. 21, 31, 35, 56, 65, 73 (1120–45); *TC* 1, 786, 859; 2, 105, 436; 3, 592, 1600; 4, 1540, 1554, 1698; 5, 212, 1532; *LGW* Prol. F 514, G 502, F 516, G 504, F 553, 1104(?). The pagan Hades is referred to as Pluto's *derke regioun* (*CT* A 2082) and *regne* (A 2299) which is *derk and lowe* ("deep") and *under ground* (F 1075). In *TC* 4, 790, it is alluded to as *ther Pluto regneth*. On various features and characteristics of this *Helle* see Theodore Spencer, 'Chaucer's Hell', *Speculum*, II (1927), 177–200.

For other underworld localities see *Flethegon, Lete, Stix.*

[**Hellespont**], "Sea of Helle" [Lat. *Hellespontus*], mod. Dardanelles, is referred to in *TC* 4, 1549, as the *se* into which the Simois (*Symois*, below) flows.

The name is based on Helle, maiden of Greek legend who drowned in the Hellespont, and Gk *póntos* "sea".

Hermus, Hermus [Lat. *Hermus*], mod. Sarabat, in antiquity known as a gold-bearing river in Aeolis (Aeolia), Asia Minor, flowing into the Gulf of Smyrna (cp. *PMLA*, XLII [1927], 670–72). In *Bo* 3, m. 10, l. 15 (960–65) it is mentioned along with the Indus and Tagus as a source of wealth; *rede brinke* (l. 16) refers to gold-bearing gravel.

Chaucer's form is Latin.

Holdernesse, Holderness Division (YER), a low-lying marshy peninsula and grain-growing district E of *Hulle* (below), is correctly described in *CT* D 1710 as a *mersshy contré* and is said to be the home of Friar John (D 2171; dimunitive *Jankin* D 2288). In *CT* D 1299 it is referred to anticipitorially as a *contré* or district, home of an anonymous Summoner and Friar, as if both the Friar and the Summoner, perhaps for effect, were laying their tales in the same locale. In the ecclesiastical district is an imaginary friary or convent of friars (*covent*) mentioned in *CT* D 1863, 1959, 1975, 2130, 2250, 2259, 2261, 2285; in D 2099, 2102 it is a *cloistre*. In this same area, the "limitation" (*NED* 2a) or circuit of the Summoner's preaching and begging friar is a *toun* (D 1778) with houses (D 1738, 1765), a *hostelrye* (D 1779) and the house of one Thomas (*hous*: D 1766, 1989, 2200) which is the scene of the main action of the tale. Muirhead *England* 520.

The name may look back to ON *höldr*, gen. sing. *höldar*, in Anglo-Saxon times the title of a high official in the Danelaw (*NED s.v.* "hold" sb. 3) and OE *ness* m. "headland, peninsula"; *DEPN s.v.*; *PN* XIV *YER* 14–15.

Hous of Dedalus, alternately Lat. *Domus Daedali,* the legendary labyrinth of Minos, king at Knossos in Crete (mod. Gk *Kandia*), is mentioned in *Bo* 3, pr. 12, l. 171 (1100–05) in connection with the elaborate scheme of entrances and exits characteristic of this structure, supposedly built by the skillful Athenian craftsman Daedalus. Though not referred to by name, it plays an important part in the "Legend of Ariadne" (*LGW* 1886 ff.), where it is commonly called a *prisoun* and its mazelike character described in *LGW* 2012–14. In *HF* 1920–21 (3, 830–31) it is, evidently for the sake of rime, once called by its Latin name *Domus Dedaly* (: *faste by*) and defined *Laboryntus* (see Skeat III, 283–84; Robinson 787, n. 1920). Related to, though said to be not half so remarkable or elaborately constructed as, the *Hous of Dedalus* is a curious structure, often referred to by the modern and non-Chaucerian designation "House of Rumor"; in fact, the word *rumour* is scarcely ever used by Chaucer. This outlying building, implicitly on Fame's manor, is one of Chaucer's most striking conceptions and is made the basis of some of his most remarkable description. The suggested relationship or similarity, if not identity, appears in *HF* 1920–23 (3, 830–33), a passage to be punctuated somewhat as follows:

> an hous. (That *Domus Dedaly,*
> that *Laboryntus* cleped ys,
> nas mad so wonderlych y-wis
> ne half so queyntelych y-wrought.)

It is a *hous* in 1925 (3, 835), 1935 (3, 845), 1942 (3, 852), 1945 (3, 855), 1977 (3, 887), 1987 (3, 897), 1989 (3, 899), 2030 (3, 940), 2121 (3, 1031); in 1996 (3, 906) it is a *place*, in 2142 (3, 1052) a *halle*. It is a central news-gathering bureau, a proto-Reuters or ur-AP, located at the foot of a cliff or hill on whose top stands the *Hous of Fame* (*q.v.*); *tydinges* "news items" is the usual word (*passim*) for what is collected and exchanged there and thence disseminated throughout the world through the agency of Fame (cp. 2111–17 [3, 1021–27]).

This fantastic *hous* is conceived as a huge, elaborately wrought (1923–24 [3, 833–34]) structure revolving at the speed of thought (1924–25 [3, 834–35])—for this and other examples of prescientific conceptions of maximum speed, see Stith Thompson, *Motif-Index of Folk Literature* III (Bloomington, Ind.-Helsinki, 1934), 339 H 632.2—and emitting a tremendously loud noise (1927–30 [8, 37–40], *swough* 1941 [3, 851], *chirkinges* 1944 [3, 854]). It is made of wickers, presumably osiers (*twigges*, 1936–37 [3, 846–47], 1941 [3, 851]), red, white, green and natural wood color (*fawle*), such as are used in making (bird)cages and baskets of various sorts (1938–40 [3, 848–50]). Its open-work character, like that of a peasant-made birdcage, is stressed: there are millions of openings: *dores open wyde* (1952 [3, 862]) *entrees* (1945 [3, 855]), *holes* (1949 [3, 859]), (2110 [3, 1020]), and windows (2029 [3, 939]), (2083 [3, 993]), (2091 [3, 1001]), all to facilitate ready passage in and out of news items, true or false, bits of gossip, and the like. It is *sixty myle of length* (1979 [3, 889]), in effect 60 m. in diameter, and despite the insubstantial material with which it was constructed was built to last (1980–81 [3, 890–91]). On various possible sources of inspiration for various parts or elements of the structure, see Robinson 787, n. 1925 ff.

Here, as in the *Boece* passage cited above, *hous* renders Lat. *domus* in a transferred and much less common sense of "building".

Hous of Fame, Castle of "Fama" or "Fame", a semi-mythological site (*HF* 1114 [3, 24]), is conceived as located on a spaceplatform of considerable area just between heaven, earth, and sea (714–15 [2, 206–07]), at a point presumed to be the center of gravity, so to speak, of the Universe. It is referred to inferentially in '*the book also of Fame*' of *CT* I 1085 [1085–90]. It is pictured as a mediaeval fortified castle on a cliff (*roche*, 1116–17 [3, 26–27] ff.) at least as high as the highest in Spain, not of stone but of ice (1130 [3, 40]) and towering above a settlement which is in a *valeye* (1918 [3, 828]) with a *strete* (1049 [2, 541]). (The highest mountain in Spain is the Pico de Aneto or Pic d'Anethou of 10,965 ft or 3404 meters in the eastern Pyrenees; it is doubtful if Chaucer knew much if anything about this and nearby peaks. He did certainly know of The Rock of Gibraltar [*Jubaltare* in *CT* B 947] whose highest point, Rock Gun, is 1349 ft and this he may well have had in mind here.) There Chaucer, having touched down after his flight through the firmament, finds himself and from there, after a good stiff climb (1118–19 [3, 28–29]), reaches the castle and ultimately Fame's *halle* or throne-room. On the remarkable structure in the valley on the outskirts of Fame's manor see under *Hous of Dedalus*, above.

In order of descending frequency Fame's residence is referred to as *hous*, *castel*, *place*, *paleys*, and *woon*. The titular designation *hous*, mostly in the combinations *Fames Hous* and *Hous of Fame* and used only a little more than halfway through the poem, is mentioned in 663 (2, 155), 786 (2, 78), 821 (2, 313),

882 (2, 374), 1023 (2, 515), 1026 (2, 519), 1064 (2, 556), 1070 (2, 562), 1105 (3, 15), 1114 (3, 24); hereafter it is a *castel* in 1161 (3, 71), 1176 (3, 86), 1185 (3, 95), 1196 (3, 106), *castel-yate* 1294 (3, 204), 1917 (3, 827), 1919 (3, 829); *place* in 662 (2, 154), 843 (2, 335), *Fames place* 1053 (2, 545), 1088 (2, 580), 1111 (3, 21), 1115 (3, 25), 1169 (3, 79); *paleys* in 713 (2, 205), 1075 (2, 567), 1090 (2, 582), *paleys-walles* 1398 (3, 308); a *woon* or dwelling in 1166 (3, 76). The existence of Fame's place is implied in 2111–17 (3, 1020–27).

The *roche* is a *hil* (1152 [3, 627], 1165 [3, 75]) of ice on whose faces are carved the names, mostly melted away by thawing, of former great men (1136–37 [3, 46–47]). At the top (*cop* 1166 [3, 76]) stands Fame's castle, whose walls are built of glistening beryl (1184 [3, 94], 1288 [3, 198]), with a *tour* (1185 [3, 95]); there are "bowers" or private apartments (1186, [3 96]) and a magnificent *halle* or great reception hall, in effect a throne-room (see below). The castle is elaborately adorned with archi-tectural ornaments (1188 [3, 98] ff.), as are the *yates* (1301 [3, 211]), presenting a picture which recalls something similar in *Sir Gawain and the Grene Knight* 767–78, where *Sayn Gilyan* (l. 774) and *bone hostel* (l. 776) likewise invite comparison—al-most surely without significance—with the eagle's "*Seynt Julyan loo, bon hostel*" of *HF* 1022 (2, 514). For some of the multitude milling about outside the castle there are seats (*sees* 1251 [3, 161]).

The *halle* is conceived as a vast throne-room in which the essential action of ll. 1341–1917 of the poem takes place. Its floor, walls, and roof are plated with gold half a foot thick (1343–46 [3, 253–56]); it is a sumptuous place and is referred to in 1356–57 (3, 266–67) as *Fames halle*, elsewhere simply as *halle* in 1186 (3, 96), 1314 (3, 224), 1342 (3, 252), 1514 (3, 424), 1527

(3, 437), 1533 (3, 443), 1568 (3, 478). High on a dais is an imperial throne made of a single ruby-red carbuncle (1360–63 [3, 270–73]) where Fame sits and dispenses her in the main uneven-handed justice. Along both sides of the hall from the dais to the wide portals (*dores wide*, 1420 [3, 334]) are statues of great historians of the past (1421 [3, 331] ff.) mounted on pedestals (*peler* 1421 [3, 33] ff.) of metal, base and noble, and of appropriate symbolism.

The designations *castel* and *paleys* for this remarkable edifice need no comment since they convey to the modern reader exactly what they conveyed to Chaucer and his audience; nor do such general terms as *place* and *woon*, but a word may be said about *hous*. Today "*house*" normally suggests a private dwelling of modest or reasonable proportions, though it is still used on occasion for a complex of buildings such as "monastic house", a university college as "the House" for Christ Church, Oxford, Peterhouse for St. Peter's College, Cambridge, the several "Houses" of Harvard University, or a humble flophouse (see *NED s.v.* "house" for these and other uses). In *HF*, however, *hous* is through about the first half of the poem used very definitely as a virtual synonym for the subsequently used *castel* and *paleys* which replace it after l. 1114 and presumably represents a survival of similar uses in Old English (Anglo-Saxon) where, perhaps most conspicuously, *hús* is used frequently in *Béowulf* to refer to the great Danish royal hall of "Heorot". It may be recalled that MHG *hús* is likewise frequently used in the *Nibelungenlied* to refer to the Burgundian royal palace of King Gunthere (see *MS*, VII [1945], 134, under *Wormez*).

Hulle, Kingston-upon-Hull, semiofficially and usually Hull (YER), an important sea (river-) port at the confluence of the little river Hull and the Humber estuary (Muirhead *England* 518–21), is mentioned in *CT* A 404 as the northern limit of a stretch of water extending to Cartagena (prov. Murcia), Mediterranean sea-port, Spain (see *Cartage* II above).

The town takes its name from the river, OE (*sío éa*) *Hull*, of Celtic origin; see *ERN* 200–01, *PN* XIV *YER* 209–10.

I

Ilio[u]n, [Lat. *Ilium*], in antiquity a poetical name for Troy (*Troie*, below) whose citadel was *Pergama* (neut. plur.) or *Pergamum* (sg.). Among mediaeval writers Pergamum was supplanted as the name of the citadel by Ilium and is so used by Chaucer. It is mentioned in *HF* 158, *LGW* 936, *CT* B 289, B *4546 (3356). It is described as the chief donjon (*dongeoun*) of Troy in *LGW* 937, similarly as a *noble tour* (*LGW* 936) and evidently as a *castel* in *HF* 163. The pairing *of Troie and of Ilyoun* in *BD* 1248 suggests that Chaucer may have thought of Ilium as an enclave, a town within Troy.

Chaucer's form looks back to OFr *Ilioun*; the whole name is based on Ilus, son of Tros, legendary eponymous of Troy.

Inde, India, answering essentially to mod. India and Pakistan [Lat. *India*], etymologically the region of the river Indus of West Pakistan (*Indus*, below), is chiefly mentioned as symbolic of a remote and distant place, somewhere far off (cp. *Caucasus*, above): so in *RR* 624; *BD* 889; *Bo* 3, m. 5, l. 6 (740–45) (*a contré*); *TC* 5, 971; *CT* C 722, D 824. It is used twice to describe tigers: *Bo* 4, m. 3, l. 17 (1315–20); *CT* E 1199. It is a realm of a legendary or imaginary king Demetrius (*CT* A 2156) and of an unnamed thirteenth-century ruler said also to rule Arabia

(*CT* F 110); in *Mars* 246 it is a source of precious stones (so *Nibelungenlied* 403, 1). It is twice mentioned with reference to the supposed scene of the missionary activities of the apostle St Thomas (shrine at Mylapur, Madras): *CT* D 1980 (*Thomas lyf of Inde*), E 1230.

Chaucer's form is based on OFr *Inde* vs mod. Fr. *les Indes*.

Indus, Lat., the Indus [Sanskrit *Sindh*], the great river of West Pakistan and source of the name "India" (*Inde*, above), rises in the Himalayas of Tibet and flows into the Arabian Sea. It is mentioned in *Bo* 3, m. 10, l. 16 (965–70) as a source of precious stones (cp. *Mars* 246) and is said (l. 17) to be *next the hote partie of the world*, perhaps with reference to the fact that it enters the Arabian Sea only a little north of the Tropic of Cancer.

Ypres [var. MR V, 40], Ieper (Fr. *Ypres*) on the Ieperleet (Fr. *Yperlée*) was in the Middle Ages along with *Brugges* and *Gaunt* one of the great towns of *West Flaundres* and, like the others, owed its prosperity to its textile industry. The magnificent Cloth Hall (Les Halles) was destroyed in World War I. It is mentioned in connection with the textile industry in *CT* A 448.

OFr *Ipre(s)* is the source of Chaucer's form and that of modern English and French. During and after World War I a pronunciation [*wiperz*] came to be commonly used in substandard English and often jocosely by Standard speakers after the first of the three great battles of Ypres in October-November 1914. Despite a not uncommon semipopular notion the word "diaper" is not based on "*drap d'Ypres*"; see *NED s.v.* "diaper".

Ispannie, gen. sing. of Lat. (*H*)*ispania*, Spain, is used in the heading before *CT* B² *3565 (2375). On this name see under *Spaigne*.

Israel, (kingdom of) Israel [Lat. *Israel*], the people descended from Jacob, called Israel ("he that strives with God", *Gen.* xxxii, 28), the Jewish or Hebrew people; cp. *Jewerie*, below. In *CT* B *3250 (2060) Sampson is said to have the rule of Israel, in B *3342 (2152) Nebuchadrezzar has male children of the royal blood of Israel castrated; in *LGW* 1880 it is a *lond*, vaguely Palestine, and is mentioned in connection with the woman of Samaria (*Samaritan*, below).

Ytacus, Lat. adj.-sb., the Ithacan [Lat. *Ithacus*], is used for Ulysses in *Bo* 4, m. 7, l. 20 (1600–05). Cp. *Narcice*, below.

Itayl[l]e, Italy, the Italian peninsula [Lat. *Italia*] is mentioned in connection with three quite different periods of Italian history

A. Most of Chaucer's references are to various phases of Aeneas' voyage from Troy via Carthage (*HF* 187, 196, 298, 430, 433; *LGW* 952, 1329), his arrival (*HF* 147, 452 cp. *Lavyne*, below), and the presaged conquest (*LGW* 1298 and cp. *Ardea*, above).

B. In *CT* B 441 *Ytaille* is the goal of Constance's ordeal when she is launched from Syria; the period is the late sixth century in the reign of Ælla, first king of Deira (later part of Northumbria, England), *regn.* A.D. 560–88.

C. The other references are to Italy of Chaucer's own time. In *CT* B *3650 (2460) the *grete poete of Ytaille* is Dante, while in E 33 Petrarch is said to illumine all Italy with his poetry. The Clerk's Tale begins in the district of Saluzzo (*Saluces*) in the west of Italy (*CT* E 57). There is delicious food in the Italy of Chaucer's day (*CT* E 266, 1714) and the country is referred to in a general way in *CT* E 1132, 1178, 1511.

The following towns and localities of mediaeval Italy are in one way or another mentioned or inferred: *Apennyn, Boloigne II, (de) Columpnis, Emele, Ferrare, Lynyan, Lumbardes. Lumbardia/-ye, Melan, Padowe, Pavye, Pemond, Pyze, Poilleys, Poo, Rome, Saluces, Venyse, Vesulus*. Cp. also *jane* and the estate or family name *Panyk*.

J

Jaconitos is mentioned in *LGW* 1590 as the capital of the district of Colchis (*Colcos*, above); in l. 1589 it is a *cyté*, in 1591 the *mayster-town* or capital, ruled by Oetes (l. 1593). Medea lives here and her *halle* is mentioned in l. 1602. Historically the chief coastal town of Colchis was Dioscuras, mod. Sukhum Kaleh.

Chaucer's name derives from Guido delle Colonne's *Iaconites ... caput regni pro sua magnitudine constituta, urbs valde pulcra*, etc.; the present form may well be a scribal error for *Jaconites*.

jane [MR VI, 360; VII, 185], a small silver coin of the great seaport town of Genoa (prov. Genova), Italy, current in England in the fourteenth century, is mentioned in *CT* B² *1925 (735) (*many a jane*) to describe the cost of Sir Thopas' robe of the material ciclaton; in E 999 it expresses the small worth (*deere ynogh a jane*) of the chatter of the hoi polloi.

The coin-name is based on OFr *Janne(s)* (also *Genes, Jeynes*), modern Fr. *Gênes*, Ital. *Genova*, looking back to the Roman name *Genua* (Holder I, 2005–07) perhaps of Ligurian origin. Cp. also ME *Janeway(s)*, *Geneway*, sb. and adj., "Geno(v)ese", native of Genoa, based on OFr *genoueis* (Engl. *Genoese*), Ital. *Genovese*. See further *NED* s.v. "jane".

Jerusalem, Jerusalem [Lat. *Hierusolyma*, n. pl. later *Hierusalem*, *Ierusalem*, n.], ancient capital of Palestine, the Holy City, is mentioned in three quite different connections:

A. The city in Biblical times. In *CT* B *3337 (2147) it is a *cité*, twice conquered by Nebuchadrezzar whose son Belshazzar in B *3386 (2196) uses vessels taken by his father from the *Temple* (B *3338 [2148]). In B *3786 (2596) Antiochus threatens vengeance on the city.

B. A goal of mediaeval pilgrims. It is mentioned in *CT* A 463, D 495. In *RR* 554 the reference is general, Jerusalem being one terminus of a long distance, chosen probably, however, because of its familiarity to pilgrims.

C. With the adj. *celestial* it refers to the "holy city, new Jerusalem" of *Apoc.* xxi, 2, in *CT* I 51, 80; in I 588 it is the *cité of a greet Kyng*.

The name is often pronounced trisyllabically (Jer'salem); for a similarly reduced pronunciation cp. Icel. *Jórsalir* (m.pl.) with popular adaptation of -*salem* to Icel. -*salir* "dwellings", common in place-names.

Jew [Jue], Jew (OFr *giu*), a person of Hebrew race (originally of the kingdom of Judah), an Israelite; cp. (*H*)*ebraik*, above.

A. With reference to the ancient Hebrews in *CT* C 351, 364 (an unidentified "holy Jew", perhaps Jacob), E 2277 (Solomon), B *3782–83 (2592–93) (Maccabean Jews of II *Macc.* 9); *HF* 1434 (3, 344) (*Jewes gestes*, i.e., Flavius Josephus' *Antiquitates*). The reference in *CT* B *1749 (559) is very general.

B. With reference to the Jews as slayers of Christ: *CT* C 475; I, 590–95, 595–600, 660–65, 885–90.

C. With reference to Asia Minor Jews of the Christian era as perpetrators of ritual murder: *CT* B *1755 (565), *1760 (570), *1763 (573), *1789 (599), *1791 (601), 1810 (620), 1819 (629), 1875 (685).

D. With reference to mediaeval European Jews as skilled armorers: *CT* B *2054 (864).

Chaucer's form, whence mod. "Jew", is of the older French type, later replaced by *juif* (see *NED s.v.* "Jew"); both French types look back to Lat. *Iudaeus*, in turn looking back ultimately to the patriarch Judah and the powerful tribe descended from the latter.

Jewerye [**Juerie**], Jewry (OFr *Juerie*, mod. *Juiverie*):

A. The land of the Jews, Judaea, here all Palestine: *HF* 1436 (3, 346) with reference to Flavius Josephus' *Antiquitates*.

B. A district of a town inhabited by Jews, a Jewish quarter but not a ghetto, first established in Venice in 1516: *CT* B *1679 (489), *1741 (551), *1782 (592).

This Jewry is in a *greet cité* (B *1678 [488]) in Asia Minor (see *Asie*), predominantly (?) Christian and governed by a *Provost* (*1819 [629]) or chief magistrate (*NED* "provost" 5). There is a church school (*scole, passim*). The Jewry, *place* in B *1791 [601], is crossed by a *strete* (B *1804 [614]) off which ran an *aley* (B *1758 [567]) where there was a privy (*privé place* *1758 [567], *pit* *1761 [571], *1796 [606], *wardrobe* *1762 [572]) into which the Jews are said to have thrown the body of the little Christian schoolboy. There was an *abbay* *1814 [624], also referred to as a *covent* (*1827 [624], *1867 [677]), and a marble tomb (*1871 [881]) where the child martyr was buried. Without

Chaucer's immediate source for the story it is not possible to say whether Chaucer might have had any particular place in mind; variant versions of this miracle are laid in Carcassone (France), Paris, Albigensian territory, Lincoln, and Toledo (Spain) (see B & D 467, 470, 475, 477, 480). See also *Lincolne*, p. 143, above.

For a striking nineteenth-century analogue to this most unpleasant story see *Mod. Lang. Notes* LXXI *(1956)*, 165-66.

Jubaltare [var. MR V, 529], Rock of Gibraltar (Span. *peñón de Gibraltar*), well-marked promontory (*Mons Calpe* of antiquity) in a British enclave in the Spanish province of Granada—since 1704 a Crown Colony—is mentioned in *CT* B 947 to define the 15 m. strait (*narwe mouth*, B 946) to which it has now given its name; Chaucer seems to have thought of it as the Strait of *Marrok*. The African side of the strait is marked by the promontory of *Septe* (*Abyla* of antiquity) which with *Mons Calpe* made up the *Herculis Columnae* or Pillars of Hercules (see *Pileer*).

The name *Jubaltare* looks back to Arab. *Djabal Tarik* (*ben Zaid*) "Mountain of Tarik (son of Zaid)", first landing place of that Moorish invader in 711 A.D., on which Chaucer's form is based. The modern name Gibraltar shows an intrusive *r(-bra-)*, parallaled in Span. *estrella* "star" vs Lat. *stella*. See *E Isl* II[1], 169.

K, see also C

Kayrrud [var. often *kynrede*, MR VI, 585] is used in *CT* F 808 to indicate the home, perhaps manor, of the Breton knight Arveragus and is said (F 801) to be not far from *Pedmark*; it has defied identification.

As a name (Tatlock 13–16) it surely answers to Welsh *caer rydd* "red fort", Breton *ker ru* "red village, house", but in the Breton of Chaucer's day *caer ruz* (*z* more or less = *ð*); if transmitted to Chaucer through a French source one would expect here *car* (or *kar*) *ru* (*Carru*). Tatlock 15 suggests not implausibly that the form *Kayrrud* may be Chaucer's effort to render a Breton *Caerruz* as he heard it rather than ever saw it written. Except for *Kérity*, harbor of Penmarch, there are no *Car-/Ker-* names in the vicinity, though such names occur in Britanny by the thousand, overwhelmingly to designate a private house or property (Longnon 1304–09). Chaucer's "Red House" may be merely the name of Arveragus' manor and invented at that.

Kent, Kent, county SE of London, through which the route of the pilgrims passed (see *Caunterbury Wey*), is mentioned in *HF* 1131, (3 41) and *CT* A 3291 to identify St Thomas à Becket whose shrine in Canterbury was the pilgrims' goal (see also *Caunterbury*). In Kent are *Bobbe-Up-and-Doun, Boghtoun, Caunterbury, Depeford, [Derteford], Grenewych, [Ospringe],* and *Rouchestre.*

Kent (OE *Cent*) looks back to primitive OE *Kanti, derived from Romano-British *Cantium, Cantii*, perhaps meaning "border country"; see *DEPN s.v.*

[Knaresborough (YWR)] on the Nidd, 17 m. NW of York with portions of John of Gaunt's castle where Richard II was imprisoned for a time in 1399 (Muirhead *England* 494), is not mentioned by Chaucer but may be implied in *CT* B 730, 786 (see also *Northumberlond*, below), for in the Constance story in Nicholas Trivet's *Chronique* it is the site of Deumylde's or Doumilde's place: *Knaresbourch* (var. *-bourth, -bourgh, -borugh*)

(B & D 172–73, also as *Knaresburgh* in John Gower's *Confessio Amantis*, ii, 943, 1001 [B & D, pp. 190–91]). There can be no question of Chaucer's not knowing that Knaresborough was the proper place for the wretched Donegild's "*court*", and one can only ask why he ignored or suppressed the name. A. C. Edwards, 'Knaresborough Castle and the *Kynges Moodres Court*', *Philological Quarterly*, XIX (1940), 306–09, explains this omission not at all implausibly on the grounds of political discretion, of Chaucer's not wanting to identify the castle of John of Gaunt, unpopular but powerful Duke of Lancaster, in any way as "the home of treason and the unnatural Donegild".

The background of the first element of Knaresborough is uncertain; *DEPN s.v.*

L

Laboryntus, see **Hous of Dedalus.**

Lacedomye, Lacidomye, Lacedaemonia (late Lat. *Lacedaemia*, class. Lat. *Lacedaemo(n)*, *-onis*, f.), south-eastern division of the Peleponnesus (mod. Morea) centering on the town of Lacedaemon or Sparta, in antiquity also called *Laconia*; the region and town appear in the late non-classical form *Lacedaeminia*. The region is mentioned in *CT* C 605 as the source of a mission to Corinth and in F 1380 as the home of fifty virgins claimed of the Lacedaemonians by their western neighbors of Messene or Messenia (*Mecene*, below). In C 1610 the region is referred to as a *contré*.

Chaucer's form would seem to be a reduction of sorts via OFr of the late form *Lacedaemonia*.

Latyn, adj. and sb., Latin [Lat. *Latinus*], adj. based on Latium the portion of ancient Italy which included Rome.

A. adj. 1. Of or pertaining to Latium or the ancient Latins or Romans: *HF* 1438 (3, 393) (*the Latyn poete, Virgile*), *Astr. Prol.* 32–42 (20–24) (*Latyn folk*).

2. Pertaining to the language of the ancient Latins or Romans: *Astr.*, Pt. 1, ch. 21, § 61 (100–08) (*Latyn tonge*).

B. absol. and as sb. The language of the Latins or ancient Romans; the Latin language *CT* A 638, B 519, 1190, *1713 (523), *4355 (3165), C 344, F 1174, I 865–70, 870–75; *Anel* 10; *TC* 2, 14; *Astr. Prol.* 32–42, 62 (5–11, 11–15).

Chaucer's form is from OFr.

Lavyne, ancient city of Lavinium [Lat. *Lavinium*] in Latium, Italy, now Pratica (prov. Lazio), near the coast and 15 m. south of Rome, defines in *HF* 148 the coastal region (*strondes of Lavyne*) where Aeneas first landed on reaching Italy (cp. *Itaylle* A, above).

The town-name is based on the personal name Lavinia, daughter of Latinus and wife of Aeneas.

Lemnoun, Lemnos [Lat. *Lemnos, -us*], mod. Lemno (Ital. *Stalimeni*), island in the Aegean (*salte se, LGW* 1462, 1510; *se* 1470, 1495), in antiquity thought of as the abode of Vulcan (Hephaestus), is mentioned in *LGW* 1463 as the home of Hypsipyle, daughter of Thoas and queen of Lemnos at the time of the Argonautic Expedition. It is an *yle* (*LGW* 1463, 1466), with a coast-line characterized by cliffs (*clyves, clyf*, 1470, 1497); Hypsipyle has a *castel* (1507), where she takes Jason and his Argonauts.

Chaucer's *Lemnoun* would seem to be OFr and based on a Lat. *Lemno, -onem*.

[**Corseynt**] **Leonard,** St Leonard (November 6th), patron
saint of prisoners, is mentioned in *HF* 117 as the saint of a shrine
two miles from Chaucer's home. Since Chaucer is here following
Jean de Meun's *Roman de la Rose* (ed. Ernest Langlois, ll.
8836–38), the whole allusion may be merely jocose and be taken
simply as a reference to the saint, but see under *Stratford-
atte-Bowe*, below, for an apparently more personal application
of the reference.

Lepe [prov. Huelva], Spain, small town *ca* 8 m. from Aya-
monte and *ca* 3 m. in from the Atlantic coast, is mentioned in
CT C 563 to define a white wine; in C 570, where it is a *toun*,
the reference is again to the wine of the place with a strong implication that it is headier than French wines imported via
The Rochele and *Burdeus.*

According to *EUI* XXX, 64, col. 2, the name looks back to
a Roman (Iberian?) *Leptis.*

Lettow [var. MR V, 6], the kingdom of Lithuania (Lith.
Lëtuvà, MLG Lettow(en), Med. Lat. *Lit[h]uania*, whence the
modern English name), in Chaucer's day embraced a large
territory S of Kurland (now part of Latvia), including Volhynia
and part of the Ukraine to the Black Sea; it is mentioned in *CT*
A 54 as a region in which the Knight had campaigned; cp. also
Pruyce and *Ruce.*

Lith. *Lëtuvà* is perhaps based on a stem represented in Lat.
lît-us "shore" and hence may signify "coastal region"; so Julius
Pokorny, *Indogermanisches etymologisches Wörterbuch*, fascicle 7
(Bern, 1953), pp. 664–65, under *lei-* "pour, flow". Chaucer's
form is obviously based on the MLG form; see Skeat V, 7,
nn. 53, 54 *ad fin.* for *Lettow* in mid-fifteenth-century English.

Lete, the Lethe, mythological river of the ancient Greek underworld (Lat. *Lethe, -es,* f.), is in *HF* 71–72 a *flood of Helle unswete* ("unpleasant"); one branch (*strem,* 1.71), flowing into the land of the Cimmerians (*Cymerie,* above), is the river on whose bank Morpheus, god of sleep, resides.

Libie, Libya [Lat. *Libya*], in ancient geography North Africa west and exclusive of Egypt, also known in Carthaginian terminology as Africa (see *Affrike,* above), was later applied to Cyrenaica. In this latter, more general sense the shore or coasts (*strondes of Libye*) are mentioned in *Bo* 4, m. 7, l. 56 (1610–15) as where Hercules slew a huge giant Antaeus, similarly in a reference to the *desert of Lybye* (*HF* 488) as comparable to the imaginary sandy waste in which the dreamer finds himself.

More often *Libie* (=*Affrike,* above) refers to Dido's realm, centering on Carthage: so in the cases of the *reyne of Libie* (*LGW* 922), the *lond of Libie* (1123), and *Libie* (959), where Aeneas arrives after his storm-tossed voyage from Troy and takes refuge in the *haven* mentioned under *Cartage,* above. In this same application it is a *contré* (*HF* 241, *LGW* 990), a *reame* (*LGW* 1281), to be defined as either of Africa, Carthage, or Libya, a *regioun* (*LGW* 995). In the country out around Carthage is a forest (*LGW* 981) teeming with game, including lions (see *Marmoryke, Pene,* below).

Chaucer's form is OFr.

Lyde, Lydia [Lat. *Lydia*], a country in ancient Asia Minor corresponding approximately to the Turkish province of Saruehan with Sardis (mod. Salihly) as its capital and legendary homeland of the Etruscans. It is used to define the kingship of Croesus, fabulously rich successor of Alyattes in 560 B.C.:

kyng of Lyde (*HF* 105, *CT* B *3917 [2727]), *of Lyde kyng* (*CT* B *4328 [3138]).

Chaucer's form is OFr.

Lydiens, sb. plur., Lydians, inhabitants of the region of Lydia (*Lyde,* above), is used in *Bo* 2, pr. 2, l. 65 (310–15) to define the kingship of Croesus.

Chaucer's form is OFr (mod. *lydien*) and, as if from Lat. **Lydianus,* is based on the regional name *Lydia.*

Lyeys [var. MR V, 6] (Graeco-Lat. *Aegae,* Cilicia, SW Asia Minor), Ayash (vilayet of Seyhan), SW Turkey in Asia, and in Chaucer's day a seaport of consequence in the kingdom of Lesser Armenia (*Armenia Minor*), is on the coast of the Gulf of Iskenderun, formerly Alexandretta. It is mentioned in *CT* A 58 in connection with Pierre de Lusignan's 1367 campaign against it (Cook 229–30), in which the Knight is said to have participated. In Chaucer's day there was still a considerable Armenian population in the area, actually a sort of Armenian enclave.

The modern name Ayash looks back to the Graeco-Lat. acc. plur. *Aegas.* Chaucer's form is French and a variant of *Layas* (cp. also Ital. *Laiazzo*) whose initial *L-* is presumably the Romanic article. See Cook 229 for a variety of forms with and without the initial *L-,* also other variants.

Lyncolne [var. *Lincolle,* MR VII, 178], Lincoln, mainly on the N bank of the Witham, county town with cathedral, is mentioned in *CT* B *1874 (648) to define the young saint ("Little St Hugh") supposedly murdered by Jews in Lincoln in 1255 (Muirhead *England* 556) and his body thrown into a well in a courtyard (now "Jews' Court") next door to the right of "The Jews' House" in Steep Hill (street). Muirhead *England* 555–60.

Lincoln (OE *Lind-cyle[e]ne*) looks back to Romano-British *lindum* "lake" (cp. Welsh *llyn*), with reference to a broadening and canalization by the Romans of the Witham at Lincoln, reflected in the Brayford (pool), and Lat. *colonia*.

Lynyan [var. MR VI, 246], Legnano (prov. Milano) on the Olona, Italy, 18 m. NW of *Melan*, is cited in *CT* E 34 to identify Giovanni da Legnano; see Robinson 709, col. 2, n. 34.

The name may look back to an older *Ledegnanum, probably Latin *Letianum from a name *Letinus (Olivieri 305), or Lat. *Leunianum* (*EI* XX, 779).

Londo[u]n, London or more precisely the City of London, now a county corporate on the N bank of the Thames, covering an area of about 680 acres, included two hills on either side of the Walbrook valley and today is included in the postal regions E.C.1–4, now a center of business and industry. London in this older, restricted sense (population *ca.* 23,000; Darby 232–33) is mentioned in a general way in *CT* A 509, A 3632, D 555, G 1012; in A 383 it defines an ale, in A 4325, H 11 it identifies Roger (Hogge) the Cook, originally a man of *Ware*, *q.v.* In A 4343, 4365 it is a *cité*, in A 4385 a *toun*, likewise in *LGW* Prol. FG 43 where it is mentioned as a place where daisies are called daisies (*dayes-yes*).

Streets and Buildings

The following account is obviously not intended for Londoners or persons familiar with the city, to whom everything here in question will be commonplace; rather it is designed for persons who may be visiting London for the first time and might like to locate quickly and view the streets and buildings Chaucer mentions in the *Canterbury Tales*.

Starting in the SW corner of the City at Fleet St near Temple Bar we find the *Temple*, E.C.4 (*CT* A 567; in A 578 *"that hous"*) as a general name of the two Inns of Court, the Middle and Inner Temple; the Outer Temple was merely a piece of ground once belonging to the Templars which early passed into private hands. Bowden 256; Muirhead *London* xlvi–vii, 216. Continuing east in Fleet St and up Ludgate Hill we come to *Sainte Poules*, old St Paul's Cathedral (E.C.4), destroyed in the Great Fire of 1666, mentioned in *CT* A 509 as a place where a country parson might find an easy and lucrative post (Muirhead *London* 244). St Paul's appears further to be implied in *parvys* (A 310), with reference to the enclosed area or court in front of the Cathedral, noted as a rendez-vous for lawyers and their clients (see Bowden 166–67, *NED* "parvis" 1, but questioned by Manly 518). In A 3318 *"Poules wyndow"* refers to traceried windows in the old cathedral, here conceived as the basis of an ornamental pattern cut out in shoe-leather, in Mediaeval Latin *calcei fenestrati* (Skeat V, 101 *ad loc.*). Continuing east on Cannon St and one block east after crossing King William St we are at Fish Hill St, E.C.3 (*Fyssh Strete*) which runs down past the Monument (to the Great Fire) to Lower Thames St near London Bridge, in C 564 (var. *Brig Strete*, *Fleet Strete*, MR VII, 66) named as a street where Spanish wine is sold. We are now in the district of the Vintry of old (*NED s.v.* b), where Chaucer grew up as a boy. Virtually at right angles to Fish Hill St and an eastward continuation of Cannon St is Eastcheap, which is almost surely referred to as *in Chepe* and in the same verse (C 564, also 569) as *Fyssh Strete* above and in the same connection; it is un-

likely here to refer to Cheapside, E.C.2 (*in Chepe*, A 4377) below. Proceeding down Eastcheap and Great Tower St we come
to Tower Hill and the Tower, E.C.3 (*Tour*), in the SE corner of
the old city, referred to in A 3256 as the site of the old Mint
(Muirhead *London* 305) where gold *nobles* were minted in the
time of Edward III (*NED* "noble" sb. 1, 2). Thoughts of the
White Tower proper, in its day a fortress, arsenal, and state
prison, may lie behind *the* (*heighe*) *tour* of Cambuys Kan in
F 176, 340. Muirhead *London* 298–305. From the Tower we
may retrace our steps to Eastcheap and King William St, then
turn north up King William St to the statue of Wellington
in front of the Royal Exchange, thence west into the Poultry
and on into the then great highway of Cheapside, E.C.2 (*in
Chepe*, A 4377), mentioned as a place where processions on
horseback, perhaps jousts, attracted the unnamed apprentice
of the Cook's Tale from his work. This same apprentice also
liked to join up with noisy processions (*revel*), quite likely
accompanying prisoners, which would start at Newgate Prison
(*Newegate*, A 4402) and continue back through Cheapside and
straight on through Cornhill to the Cornhill prison called "the
Tun" (Skeat V, 130 *ad loc.*, and *NED* "tun" sb. 5, for later
references). On the background and etymology of many of these
streets and sites see Eilert Ekwall, *Street-Names of the City
of London* (Oxford, 1954), Index, pp. 205 ff., and fold-out map
at end, also the note on the map, p. vi.

Not identifiable are general references to food-shops (A 4352,
4376, 4395, 4410 [*place*], 4422), taverns in A 4375, miscellaneous
dwellings in G 1023, 1217, and nooks and corners and blind
alleys (*hernes and lanes blynde*) in G 658.

For other parts of the London area mentioned by Chaucer
see *Depeford, Eltham, Grenewych, Sheene, Southwerk, Stratford-*

*atte-Bowe, Wateryng of Seint Thomas, [Westminster, City of],
Windesore.*

Loreyn[e], Lorraine [Med. Lat. *Lotharingia*, Germ. *Loth-
ringen*, OFr *Loherrei[g]ne*] in Chaucer's day referred to the Duchy
of Upper Lorraine and is mentioned in *RR* 766, 767 (*Roman de
la Rose* 750–51) to define certain songs sung at a festive party
in the Garden of the Rose in the company of Sir Myrthe.
See Ernest Langlois, *ed. cit.*, II, 302, n. 750–51, for another
reference to Lotharingian songs.

The name looks back to the Germanic (Frankish) personal
name *Chlodacharius*, later appearing as *Lothari regnum*, in turn
yielding OFr *Loherreigne* and later forms; see Gröhler II, 326,
s.v. "*Chlodachar*".

Lumbardes, Lombards, natives of *Lumbardia, Lumbardye*,
are mentioned in *CT* B² *1557 (367) as bankers living in *Parys*.
The ethnic name is based on the regional name *Lumbardye*.

Lumbardia, Lombardy [Ital. *Lombardia*] in the Latin heading
before *CT* B² *3589 (2399) is used to define (Lat.) Barnabus
(i.e., Bernabò Visconti). On this name see *Lumbardye*, below.

Lumbardye [var. MR VI, 250–51], Lombardy (Ital. *Lombardia*), territorial division of Italy including an area extending
N to the Alps, S from the Ligurian Apennines, and bounded
on the S by *Emele*, and on the W by *Permond*, including the
cities of *Melan, Pavie*, and *Saluces*. In *CT* E 46 western *Lumbardye* is said to be bounded by the *Apennyn* and is also referred
to in E 945; the region in general is mentioned in E 72, 1245.
In *CT* B² *3590 (2400) it is used to define Bernabò Visconti of

Melan as the scourge of the region; the same note is struck in *LGW* F 374 (G 354), where Alcestis urges the god of love not to be like *tirauntz of Lumbardye*.

Lumbardia, Lumbardye, "the land of the Langobards, Lombards", is a regional name in *-ia*, based on the Germanic tribal name (Lat.) *Lango-Bardi* "long beards" whose ultimate home was in the Jutland peninsula, Denmark. On this tribal name see *Reallexikon* III, 123–25; Olivieri 315–16; Matthias 124–30. Chaucer's and the modern English forms are based on French.

lussheburghe [var. MR VII, 470], lushburg (*NED s.v.*), a counterfeit coin imitating an English silver penny, was imported from Luxemburg in the reign of Edward III and gave rise to a word with the general sense of counterfeit money; these coins are mentioned in *CT* B² *3152 (1926) as a base coin with which, figuratively speaking, the clergy did not pay in connection with love-affairs (see Robinson 745, n. 1926).

The word, like the name of the place from which it is derived, is an anglicization of sorts of the Duchy, now Grand Duchy of Luxembourg (Du., Germ. *Luxemburg*, older *Lützelburg*, Ital. *Lussemburgo*), a name based on the designation of the tenth-century ducal castle, *lucilin, -un burch* and the like (dat. sing.) "(at) the little stronghold"; cp. other German Lützelburgs.

M

Macedo, Lat. n. sg., a Macedonian, inhabitant of Macedon (see *Macedoyne*, below), in *HF* 915 (2, 407) identifies Alexander the Great and as in the case of the Lat. adj. *Delphicus* (above) is used for reasons of rhyme (: *Scipio*). Cp. also *Tyro*, below.

Macedoyne, Macedonye, Macedonia, Macedon [Lat. *Macedonia*], a region of varying limits north of the Aegean Sea between Thessaly (*Tessalie*, below) and Thrace (*Trace*, below), homeland of the *Macedones* (see *Macedo*, above), is in *BD* 1062 (cp. 1060) thought of as a region of great wealth and in *CT* B *3846 (2656) identifies as father of Alexander the Great, Philip, under whom Macedonia first became powerful. In *CT* F 1435 *oon of Macedoyne* stands for "a Macedonian".

Chaucer's forms look back, on the one hand, to the semi-learned OFr *Macedonie*, on the other to the more popular type *Macedoine* (mod. Fr. *Macédoine*), familiar in Mod. English as a culinary term to describe a mixture of cut-up fruits or vegetables.

Mantoan [Lat. *Mantuanus*], Mantuan, pertaining to Mantua (mod. Mantova, prov. Mantova), ancient Etruscan city of Gallia Transpadana built on an island in the Mincio. In *LGW* 924 it is used to describe Virgil, whose birthplace was at Andes near Mantua where he later long resided.

Mantoan (for *Mantuan*) is a more or less learned adaptation of the Lat. adj.; cp. *Theban, Tholosan, Trojan,* below.

Marmoryke, Marmarica [Lat. *Marmarica*], in ancient geography a region on the north coast of Africa between Egypt and Cyrenaica, the eastern part of Barca or Benghasi, is in *Bo* 4, m. 3, l. 13 (1310–15) a *contré* in which there are lions; for other North African lions see *Libie*, above, and *Pene*, below.

Chaucer's form is OFr.

Marrok [var. MR V, 484), Morocco (Fr. *Maroc*, Span. *Marruecos*, Ital. *Marocco*, Arab. *al-Maghrib al-Aqsa*], now an

independent kingdom of NW Africa with coasts on the Medi-
terranean and the Atlantic, is mentioned in *CT* B 465 to define
Strayte (B 464), i.e., the Strait of Gibraltar (see *Jubaltare*,
Septe), through which Custance passed on her involuntary
voyage to England; see also *Pileer*, below. In Chaucer's day
Marrok was virtually coextensive with *Bel-Marye*, which with
Algeria constituted the Arab. *al-Djazira al-Maghrib* "The
Island of the West" ("island" with reference to being bounded
by the Atlantic and the Mediterranean) or now *al-Maghrib al-
Aqsa* "The Far West", comprising NW Africa.

Chaucer's form is French, the unexpected, irregular first *o* of
the modern English name being perhaps due to the influence
of the word "Moor". The name looks back to Arab. *Marrakash*,
city of W. Central Morroco, extended to include the whole
region of which it was the ancient capital; *Marrok* and the like
show western abbreviatory truncation of the final *-ash*.

Mecene, Messene or Messenia [Lat. *Messene, -es*, f.] is a
district and town in the SW Peloponnesus, whose people, *hem
of Mecene*, are mentioned in *CT* F 1379 in connection with a
mission to neighboring Lacedaemon (*Lacedomye*, above).

Medes, the Medes [Lat. *Medi*], people of ancient Media in
NW Iran, here viewed as united with the Persians (*Perces*,
below), are mentioned in *CT* B *3425 (2235) together with the
Persians as a people who will take over the Assyrian kingdom
centering on Babylon (*Babiloigne*, above), ruled by Belshazzar,
son of Nebuchadrezzar.

Chaucer's form is OFr, based on Lat. acc. pl. *Medos*.

[Mediterranean Sea], generally speaking the sea which
separates Europe from Africa and extends from Palestine to

the Strait of Gibraltar (*Pileer of Hercules*, below), is in *RR* 2748, *BD* 140, *CT* A 59 *the Gre(e)te Se(e)*; in *CT* B 464 the *See of Greece*. Elsewhere it is a *se*, occasionally with the conventional epithet *salte*: *BD* 67, 69, 208; *HF* 238, 255; *Bo* 4, m. 3, l. 3 (1310–15); *LGW* 950, 953, 958, 1048, 1188, 1278; *CT* B 445.

Melan [var. MR VII, 511], Milan (Ital. *Milano*, Germ. *Mailand*) on the Olona, on the Lombard plain, Italy, is mentioned in *CT* B² *3489 (2399) to define Bernabò Visconti.

The name looks back to Gaulish *Mediolānum* "central point on the (Lombard) plain", with reference to Milan's geographical position, > *Meialāno (cp. OE *Mǽʒelan*) > *Meilāno, whence with reduction of the diphthong > Ital. *Milano*. See WP II, 61 near bottom; Holder II, 467–521; Matthias 132; Gröhler I, 129–30 for many examples in Gaulish territory of this widespread name-type. The name appears in Old Icelandic as *Mélans borg* (*MS* VI, 335). Chaucer's form reflects the common OFr type *Meland*, *Melanz* (cp. Germ. *Mailand* and Matthias 132–36) vs modern Fr. *Milan*.

Melesie, Miletus [Lat. *Miletus*], mod. Palatia (?), a town in ancient Caria (Asia Minor) on the Latmic Gulf nr the mouth of the Maeander river (mod. Mendere su), is mentioned in *CT* F 1409 in connection with the sack of the town in 276 B.C. by the Gauls (*Gawle*, above).

Chaucer's form is OFr (Mod. Fr. *Milet*) and as if from a Lat. *Miletia*.

Mercen-rike, kingdom of the Mercians, Mercia, mentioned in *CT* B *4302, (3113) as the kingdom of Kenulphus (OE

Cǽn-wulf, regn. 796–821), father of little St Kenelm (OE *Cǽn-helm*). At the time in question Mercia embraced an area lying roughly between the Ribble and the Humber in the north to the Thames and the mouth of the Severn in the south, exclusive of East Anglia.

The normal OE designation of Mercia is *Mierćna land* "land of the Marchmen", in Latin *Merciorum regio* and the like; the OE form might have been expected to yield a later East Midland *Merchen-lond* or *-riche* (OE *ríće*). Chaucer's *rike* is Scandinavian (ON *ríki*) and northern (see *NED* "riche"), and the *k* of *Merc-* (vs *Merch-*) may likewise very well reflect Scandinavian influence. But the difficulty does not end here, for the overwhelming majority of the manuscripts (MR VII, 581) read *Merten-*, several with distorted spellings but showing a *t*, plus a miscellany of utterly wild forms. Only the Paris Ms. reads *Merkenryk*. Whatever Chaucer knew about this name or thought about it, it is only too apparent that later scribes either assumed a region *Merten-rike* or went completely to pieces when faced with their exemplars at this point.

Middelburgh [var. MR V, 23], Middelburg, prov. Zeeland, near Flushing (Du. *Vlissingen*, Fr. *Flessingue*), on the island of Walcheren at the mouth of the Schelde, Holland, is mentioned in *CT* A 277 as the Continental terminus of a 125 m. stretch across the North Sea to *Orewelle* (see below) in Suffolk, England, which the Merchant wanted kept open for trade at all costs.

The name is of obvious derivation and means the "central stronghold or fortification", so-called because of its central position on the island of Walcheren. Chaucer's form is adapted from Dutch.

N

Narice, Mt Neritos [Lat. *Neritos, -us*] on the small Ionian island of Ithaca (popularly Thiaki, see *Ythacus*, above), home of Ulysses, hence poetically here for the island itself. In *Bo* 4, m. l. 2 (1310–15) it is a *contré* of which Ulysses is *duc*.
The Latin caption to Chaucer's version of Boethius' meter reads "*Vela Naricii ducis*" for "*Neritii ducis*" of Boethius; on this slightly corrupted form (with the common scribal confusion of *t* and *c*) of the Lat. adj. *Neritius* "pertaining to Neritos, Ithacan" Chaucer has based his form of the name.

[Naxos, older **Dia**], mod. Naxia, Axia, Aegean island of the Cyclades, not named directly, is referred to as an *yle* and as the place where Ariadne, daughter of King Minos of Crete, was abandoned by Theseus of Athens (*HF* 416, *LGW* 2163, 2167). In *HF* 417 it is *desert* (uninhabited) and *CT* B 68 *bareyne* (desolate), in *LGW* 2168 it is a *lond*, in *LGW* 2189 the shore (*stronde*) is mentioned, also caves (*holwe rokkes*, 2193) and a cliff (*rokke*, 2195).

Nazarenus, Lat. adj., Nazarene, of or pertaining to Nazareth, mod. En-Nasira, a town of Palestine and home of the parents of Jesus Christ and place of Jesus' early childhood. It is mentioned in *CT* I, 283 (*John* xix, 19) to define Jesus disparagingly; in I 288 the name is etymologized "flourishing" (see Robinson p. 768 n. 288.).

[The] Newe Toun is used in *CT* G 1428 to define the alchemist Arnaldus de Villanova (1235–1312?), supposedly author of the *Rosarie* (*NED s.v.* "rosary", 1) or *Rosarium Philosophorum* of F 1429, cited by Chaucer in error for the former's *de Lapide*

Philosophorum (Robinson 762, n. 1428). The name-type "new settlement" is widespread (cp. Gröhler II, 33 ff.) and Newton's, Neuburg's, Villanova's, Villanueva's, Villeneuve's (see Longnon Nos. 515–16) abound in the world. As in the case of *Drye See* Chaucer is merely translating a foreign place-name, here Lat. *Villanova*, and quite likely had no idea of, nor interest in, its identification. In actuality it is not improbably Villeneuve-Loubet, formerly Villeneuve-les-Vence in Provence (dép. Alpes-Maritimes), France; see René Verrier, *Etudes sur Arnaud de Villeneuve* (Leyden, 1947), esp. pp. 26, 42.

Nyneve[e], Nineveh, long the capital of ancient Assyria, on the east bank of the upper Tigris (*Tigrys*, below), is mentioned in *BD* 1063 (cp. l. 1060) as representative of great wealth, and in *CT* G 974, along with Rome, Alexandria in Egypt, and Troy, as a very large city. In *CT* B 487 it is referred to as the site of Jonah's delivery to dry land from the stomach of a fish (*Jon*, ii, 1, 10). Mosul (Iraq) is across the river from the ancient sites.

North contre, the North country, essentially England north of the Humber (*NED s.v.*), is mentioned in *CT* D 1413 by the devil (alias a forester or bailiff) as his home ("*fer in the North contré*"). Reference thus to the north may have been intended by Chaucer, and conceivably so understood by his readers, as an oblique allusion to the infernal regions; see Robinson 705, n. 1413. In the frame-work of the Friar's Tale, however, I suspect that it was just understood as it would be understood today, namely, as the North country.

Northfolk, the county of Norfolk in East Anglia, mentioned in *CT* A 619 (var. MR V, 58) to identify *Baldeswelle* (*q.v.*), home of Oswald the Reeve. Also in Norfolk is *Bromeholm*.

The name looks back to OE *Norþ-folc* "people settled in the north" (of East Anglia vs the people designated as *Súþ-folc*, modern Suffolk).

[**North Sea**], see *See* under *Flaundres, Middelburgh.*

Northumberlond, despite the form, this name does not historically refer here at all to Northumberland, small, most northerly eastern county, separated from Berwickshire, Scotland, by the Tweed, but to the far earlier Anglian kingdom of Deira. It is mentioned in *CT* B 578 as the kingdom of Alla (OE *Ælla, regn.* 560–588). This ancient kingdom, joined with Bernicia sometime after Ælla's death to form the large kingdom of Northumbria, included roughly the counties of Yorkshire (East and West Riding) and Lancashire. One may properly ask oneself, however, whether Chaucer in telling the "Northumberland' episode in the Man of Law's Tale knew of, or cared about, such historical matters; to him Northumberland may have meant the kingdom of Northumbria but perhaps even more likely the modern county, whose coast is his principal concern. The region is correctly said to be pagan (B 534, 540, 545) though a few Late British Christians linger on in B 547 (?). In B 508 the region is mentioned as where the sea cast Custance ashore. Alla's kingdom is referred to as a *lond* in B 522, 540, 604, 828, 862, as a *contré* in B 534, 541, and as his *regne* in B 735, 797. The coast is conspicuous and is referred to as *sond* in B 509, *stronde* in B 825, 864, *plages* "beaches" in B 542. The North Sea is *our wilde see* in B 506, 526, 557, 875, 902; in B 505 it is an *occian*. There is a castle or fortress in a town on or near the coast and is in charge of a governor or warden (*Constable, NED s.v.* 3b): *hold* "stronghold" B 507, *castel* 512, 550, 807, 878; it is called the *kinges hoom* in B 874, 876, and is said to be a *toun* in B 587, a *place* in B 575(?). The *court* of wicked Donegild, Alla's mother, of B 786 and implied in B 730, was presumably conceived by Chaucer as being at *Knaresborough, q.v.*

The name looks back to OE *Norþ-hymbra land* "land of people living north of the Humber".

O

Occian, in antiquity the sea or waters surrounding the known world of Europe, Africa, and Asia (Lat. *Oceanus*), is in effect the Atlantic Ocean and the North Sea. It is mentioned in *Bo* 4, m. 6, ll. 15–16 (1550–55) as *the see of the Occian* and *the See*, in ll. 13–14 it is *the Westrene See*, said to be where the stars set; so, too, in *Bo* 4, m. 5, l. 7 (1430–35). In *CT* B 505 *oure Occian* refers to the Atlantic Ocean between the Strait of Gibraltar and England; in B 506 *oure wilde see* may refer to the English Channel. It is *see* in *TC* 5, 1815–16 (*se*) and in *Bo* 3, m. 5, l. 7 (740–45) with reference to the North Atlantic where *Tyle* (see below) is located.

Oyse, the Oise, flowing from the Belgian frontier to join the *Sayne* at Conflans-Ste-Honorine some 40 m. below *Parys*, is mentioned in *HF* 1928 (3, 838) as one limit, of which *Rome* (*Rome* "C") is the other, of a great distance over which one could have heard the noise coming out of the House of Rumor (see *Hous of Dedalus*).

The name may look back to Gaulish *Isara* (Holder II, 72–74), yielding *Eise*, later *Oise*; see Longnon No. 700 (*Pontoise*), 729.

Oreb, Mt Oreb or Horeb, is in the Bible the less usual designation of Mt Sinai (*Synay*, below); originally two different mountains may have been intended. In *CT* D 1891 it is a *mount* and is mentioned in connection with Elijah's fast of forty days and forty nights (I *Kings* xix, 8).

Orewelle, almost surely Orwell Haven (Sf), a fine and well-known anchorage at the mouth of the Orwell estuary, the sea reach of the Gipping, off Landguard and more or less opposite Harwich (Ess), has been much used from early times to the present day; Manly 514 properly refers to it as a harbor. It is mentioned in *CT* A 277 as the English terminus of the 125 m. stretch across the North Sea (formerly also the Flemish, German Ocean) to Middelburg, capital of the Dutch province of Zeeland, near Flushing (Dutch Vlissingen), which the Merchant wanted kept open for trade at all costs. The harbor is praised by Michael Drayton in his *Poly-Olbion* (1612, 1622), Song XIX, ll. 155–60 (J. W. Hebel, ed., *The Works of Michael Drayton*, IV [Oxford, 1933], p. 401). On Orwell Haven past and present see Alker Tripp. *Suffolk Sea-Borders* (London, 1926), p. 178–96 (Chap. IV: "Seaward from Orwell Haven"); Darby 301, n. 1, also 'Orwell Haven in the *Anglo-Saxon Chronicle*', *Mod. Lang. Rev.*, L (1955), 44–45.

The OE name of the estuary seems to have been *Arwe* (gen. *Arwan*) but any development to ME *Ore-* seems to be fraught with difficulties, unless Scandinavian influence is assumed. See *ERN* 311–12, with early references to Orwell Haven, including the present Chaucer passage.

Orkades, the Orcades [Lat. *Orcades*], the Orkneys, Orkney Islands (Icel. *Orkneyjar*), co. of Orkney, Scotland, a group-name including at present 29 inhabited islands, are mentioned in *TC* 5, 971, as one terminus of a long distance; cp. *Caucasus*, *Inde*, above.

The ancient name is based on a Celtic ethnic name *Orcoi "the Boars" or directly from an Old Celtic substantive reflected in Old Irish orc "(young) pig" from a fancied resemblance of these low-lying islands to a herd of swine. In Viking times this name was reformed by the Norwegians on the basis of ON orkn "grey seal" and eyjar "islands".

Orliens, Orléans on the Loire (dép. Loiret), France, in Chaucer's day the center of a duchy, is mentioned in CT F 1118 essentially as the seat of the university (Robinson 724, n. 1118) where Arveragus' anonymous brother had studied in his youth and where he had noticed a book on "natural magic" (F 1124–25) and where he hoped to track down (F 1153) some old chum.

The name looks back to the Roman gentile name Aurelia, whence *Aurelianum, later Aurelianis; Gröhler I, 235. The coincidental relationship of the name Aurelius/Aurelie, Breton knight and wooer of Dorigen, to the background of the name Orliens would, of course, have been unnoticed by Chaucer.

Osneye, Osney village (O), a suburb of Oxford W of the railway and about $\frac{1}{2}$ m. W of the town with the remains of an Augustinian priory founded in 1129 (Muirhead England 267), is mentioned in CT A 3274, 3400, as the place where a carpenter John used to go on business; in A 3659 it is said that the parish-clerk once went there. The chirche of A 3663 is Osney Abbey, and a cloisterer or monk of the same is mentioned in A 3661. Somewhere near Osney is a grange (A 3668) or outlying farmhouse, presumably thought of as belonging to the Abbot of Osney, where it is suggested untruthfully that John the carpenter may be staying for a day or two to get for the Abbot some timber stored there (A 3666–67).

The name looks back to OE *Ósan-íeʒ* "Ósa's island, or land in the midst of marshes and the like"; *PN* XXIV *O* 22.

[**Ospringe, K**], Ospringe (: *binge, hinge*), a village on the *Caunterbury Wey* (*q.v.*) ½ m. W of Faversham and a little more than 47 m. from *Southwerk*, is not mentioned by name but was in the Middle Ages, along with [*Derteford*] and *Rouchestre*, a suitable overnight stopping place on the *Caunterbury Wey* (*q.v.*) for Canterbury pilgrims and must have been the site of the *hostelrye* of *CT* G 589. Furnivall 29; Skeat V, 415–16, n. 555, also p. 418, n. 589; Littlehales 34–35; Jerrold 415, Tatlock 483 and n. 2; Robinson 760, n. 556. A not very likely suggestion that the overnight stop in question might have been at Faversham was made by one "Hermentrude", 'Chaucer's Pilgrimage', *Notes and Queries*, 8th Series, I (June 25th, 1892), 522–23. Muirhead *England* 22.

The name probably looks back to OE **or-* or **of-spryng* (not *spring*) "spring, source"; *DEPN s.v.*

Oxenford, Oxford, episcopal see and university town, is mentioned in *Astr* Pr. 12 (1–5), Pr. 121–22 (20–25), pt. II, § 22 (head.), l. 6 (245–51), § 25, l. 28 (266–70) in connection with its latitude, in *CT* A 3187 as a town. In *CT* A 285, D 527, E 1 it defines Oxford students, and in A 3329 a style of dancing. In A 3334, 3846 it is a *toun*. A (*paryssh-*)*chirche*, one of well over a score in mediaeval Oxford, is mentioned in A 3307, 3312, a *chirche*, perhaps the same, in A 3429. The adjuration to "*Seinte Frydeswyde*" in A 3448 would recall the Augustinian Priory of St Frideswide, now the site of Christ Church College; friars in the chancel of St Frideswide are mentioned in A 3656. John the carpenter's dwelling is a *hous* (A 3356, 3484, 3669, 3694) or *in* (A 3547) and has a *(shot-)wyndowe* or casement window, central to the action of the story and mentioned in A 3358, 3676, 3695, 3708, 3727, 3740, 3801; here he took in lodgers (A 3188), including the Oxford student "*hende Nicholas*" (A 3199), a point that reminds one of the small number of students who at that time lived in a college. Muirhead *England* 245–68.

OE *Oxna-ford* "ford where oxen can cross" referred specifically to Hinksey; *PN* XXIV *O* 19.

P

Padowe (var. MR V, 245), Padua (Ital. *Padova*, Fr. *Padoue*) on the Bacchiglione, Italy, home of Livy and site of an old and famous university, is mentioned in *CT* E 27 as a place where Chaucer's Clerk learned his tale from Petrarch (1304–74). Much of Petrarch's later life was spent in Padua and one of his last compositions was his Latin translation of Boccaccio's tale of Griselda, probably made at Arqua (Petrarca) *ca* 15 m. SW of Padua, where he ended his life in retirement.

The name looks back to Rom. (Venetic?) *Patavium*; Chaucer's form is French, the modern English name being taken directly from Italian; see also Matthias 151–53.

Palatye (var. MR V, 7) (Med. Lat. *Palatia*), Balat, town and vilayet in Anatolia (Turk. *Anadolu*), Turkey in Asia, is mentioned in *CT* A 65 to define the ruler or emir (*lord*) of the Seljuk Turks with whom the Knight is said to have served.

Med. Lat. *Palatia* is apparently based on Lat. *palatium* in the extended sense of any royal residence, here perhaps signifying "region of palaces", so-called from ruins in the vicinity (Cook 235). Arabic *Balat* is a wide-spread place-name thought to

represent a hybrid compounded of Lat. *palatium* and Gr.
platea "public square"; see *E Isl* I, 615–16. Chaucer's form is Fr.

Palymerie, Palmyra (Lat. *Palmyra, -ira*), in antiquity a city
and great trading-center, was situated on an oasis 150 m. east
of Damascus (*Damyssene*, above) and in the late third century
A.D. especially flourished under the Palmyrene prince Odae-
nathus (*dux Orientis*, d. 267 A.D.) and under his relict, Queen
Zenobia, enjoyed a state of formal independence of Rome. It
is the Tadmor of 2 *Chron.* viii, 4 (probably an error for Tamar)
and is still so known among the Arabs. It is mentioned in *CT*
B *3437 (2247) with reference to Queen Zenobia; in B *3545
(2355) it is a *lond*, in B *3518 (2328) as "realms" (*regnes*), while
in B *3462 (2272) it is a *contré*.

Chaucer's form, based on OFr, shows the development of a
parasitic vowel (*i, y*) between the *l* and *m*.

Panyk [var. MR VI, 313–14, 334, 353], Ital. Panico, is in
CT E 590, 764, 939 used to define the Marquis Walter's sister
and brother-in-law in whose charge Walter placed for many
years his and Griselde's daughter and son. In E 589, 763, 939
it is implied that the Earl and Countess live in or near *Boloigne*
II. Chaucer's *Panyk* is an obvious adaptation of Petrarch's Lat.
de Panico (B & D 314, 47; 324, 1: *Panici comes*, matching *de
Paniquo* of the French text), defining an old and once important
countship (*famiglia comitale*). In the thirteenth and fourteenth
centuries the earls or *conti di Panico* (*EI* XXVI, 195) constituted
a serious threat to the expansion of the commune of Bologna
(*Boloigne* II) but were finally brought to heel and obliged to live
within the city.

Boccaccio gives the name in a dialectal form with *g* for *c* as

Panago, still reflected in the little town *Borgo Panigale* some 3 m. NNW of Bologna. This family name is very likely to be identified with the grain *panico* (Lat. *panicum*) "panic-grass" (*NED s.v.*) or so-called Italian millet, perhaps once intensively grown in the area; see, for example, Holder II, 926–27, especially his final quotation from Isidore of Seville. Chaucer's form is probably an *ad hoc* anglicization either of Petrarch's *de Panico* or *de Paniquo* of the French text. In "Chaucer's 'Panik' (*Clerk's Tale*, 590)", *Mod. Lang. Notes*, LXVII (1952), 529–31 (with many interesting references), Robert B. Pearsall is not quite right (p. 530) in describing this as "a very real place"; as is said above, it is a *fundus* or estate-name applicable to a family or to define a castle belonging to a family.

Parys [var. MR V, 11; VI, 70; VII, 115, 140, 144] (dép. Seine), chief city of *Fraunce*, is mentioned as a center of banking activity in *CT* B² *1522 (332) *1556 (366). It is the site of an abbey in B² *1247 (57) and B² *1513 (323), whose existence is implied in B² *1527 ff. (337 ff.) where a priest Dan John is stationed; the abbot is mentioned in B² *1253 (63). In B² *1525 (335) it is a *toun*. In *CT* D 678 it is mentioned as being near the site (until 1129 A.D.) of the nunnery of Héloise in the suburb of Argenteuil (Seine-et-Oise), 5 m. NW of Paris (*nat fer from Parys*). In *CT* A 126 it is used to describe the *Frenssh* of the city, namely "francien", the speech of the Ile de France, where this is contrasted with whatever French the Prioress may be supposed to have natively spoken (see *Stratford-atte-Bowe*). In *RR* 1654 (*Roman de la Rose* 1620–21) Paris is linked with *Pavye* as a place of great attraction, though less so than the Garden of the Rose.

The name looks back to the Gaulish tribal name *Parisii* (Holder II, 932–47), perhaps meaning "bold ones", whose chief town *Lucotetia*, also shortened to *Lutetia* (Holder II, 301–02), was rather early renamed on the basis of the tribal name (cp. *Arras*); Gröhler I, 85–86, Longnon No. 404.

Parnaso, Pernaso [Hil, Mount of], Mount Parnassus, mod. Luakura [Lat. *Parnassus*], a mountain-range, mainly in Phocis, was viewed as holy and with Delphi (*Delphos*, above) as a home of the Muses (see *Elicone*, above). In this latter connection it is mentioned in *HF* 521 (2, 13), *Anel* 16 (with particular reference to Polyhymnia), *TC* 3, 1810 (*In Hil Pernaso*) and *CT* F 721 (*Mount of Pernaso*).

Chaucer's form looks back to Ital. *Parnaso*.

Parthes, Parthians [Lat. *Parthi*], a Scythian people of Parthia (Lat. *Parthia*, mod. Kohistan "highlands", applied to several districts west of the *Indus*), formed the nucleus of the later great Parthian Empire, often at war with Rome; their history is much involved with that of the Medes and the Persians. They are mentioned in *Bo* 2, pr. 7, l. 73 (540–45) as a people who in the time of Cicero (106–43 B.C.) feared Rome; in *CT* C 622 there is mention of an unidentified *kyng of Parthes* who gives a present of gaming dice to one Demetrius of uncertain identity and in a perhaps purely legendary situation.

Pathmos [Lat. *Patmos, -us*, f.], mod. Patmo or Patino, was in Roman times a place of exile, to which St John the Evangelist was sent and where he is said to have written the *Apocalypse* (*Revelations*); in this connection it is mentioned in *CT* B *1773 (583).

Chaucer's spelling shows an ornamental, silent *h*.

Pavye, Pavia [Rom. [Ligurian?] *Ticinum*, Holder II, 1836–40] at the juncture of the Ticino ánd the *Poo*, Italy, is mentioned in *RR* 1654 (*Roman de la Rose* 1620–21) along with *Parys* as a place of great attraction though less so than the Garden of Rose. In *CT* E 1246 it is the birthplace of the sixty-year-old knight of the Merchant's Tale, where the town is correctly said to be in *Lumbardye* (E 1245).

Forms *Papia*, *Papiae*, of uncertain origin, appear first in the ninth century; see Olivieri 416–17, Matthias 156–57.

Pedmark [var. MR VI, 584–85], most likely a distorted form of the Breton village of Penmarch (dép. Finistère) or perhaps an attempted phonetic spelling of the same, is mentioned in *CT* F 801 as being not far from the home of Arveragus, himself said to be from the uncertain *Kayrrud*; see Robinson 723, n. 801. Today a small village, Penmarch once rivalled Nantes as a seaport.

The Breton name *Penmarc'h* looks back to Breton *pen* "head" and *marc'h* "horse" and presumably referred to a rock-formation on the Pointe de Penmarch thought to resemble a "horse's head". The spelling *Ped-* vs *Pen-* predominates in the Chaucer manuscripts and must be viewed as Chaucer's form, possibly his effort to represent a later voiceless *n;* so tentatively Tatlock 1–2, n. 2. See also Longnon No. 1345.

Pemond [var. MR VI, 247], Piedmont (Ital. *Piemonte*, Fr. *Piémont*), region in NW Italy crossed by the upper valley of the *Poo*, is mentioned in *CT* E 44, though wrongly, as if Petrarch had referred to it in the proem to his Latin translation of Boccaccio's tale of Griselda (B & D 296). On the gradual growth in the extent of this region see *EI* XXVII 185–86.

This regional name, not used in antiquity, first appears in the early thirteenth century and is evidently based on a pattern answering to Lat. *ad pedem Montium* "at the foot of the Mountains (i.e., the Cottian Alps)"; for forms such as *Pedemontium*, *Pedemontana regio* see Matthias 160. Chaucer's form is adapted from OFr.

Pene, Punic land, Carthage [Lat. *Poenus*, a Phoenician, Carthaginian] is mentioned in *Bo* 3, m. 2, l. 10 (655–60) as the *contré of Pene* with reference to tame Libyan or Carthaginian lions (cp. *LGW* 1214); for more North African lions see *Libie*, *Marmoryke*, above.

Through a French intermediary the form would seem to be based on the Latin ethnic name *Poeni* "Carthaginians".

Perces, Persians, inhabitants of the empire of ancient Persia, mod. Iran (Lat. *Persae* pl. "Persians", also sg. *Perses, -ae*), are mentioned in *CT* B*3425 (2235) in conjunction with the *Medes* (above).

The form is OFr, based on Lat. acc. pl. *Persas*.

Percien, adj. and sb.

A. adj. Persian, of or pertaining to the ancient empire of Persia (Iran) (cp. *Perses*, above), in *CT* D 2079 defines Cyrus the Great (d. 529 B.C.), founder of the Persian Empire.

B. sb. pl. *Persiens* "Persians" are mentioned in *CT* B*3438 (2248) and *3536 (2346) as nationals familiar with Queen Zenobia of *Palymerie* (above) and her sons, of royal Persian descent.

In *Bo* 2, pr. 2, l. 73 (310–15) *Percyens*, appearing in the phrase *kyng of Percyens* (from Fr. *le roi de Perse*), is an error for Perses or Perseus III of Macedonia, defeated by the Romans in 186 B.C.

Percien from OFr looks back to Lat. *Persianus*, based on Lat. *Persia*.

Pernaso, see **Parnaso,** above.

Philipenses, Lat. nom. plur. adj., Philippians, citizens of Philippi (Lat. *Philippi*), city of Macedonia (*Macedoine*, above) 73 m. ENE of Saloniki, is mentioned in *CT* I 598 with reference to St Paul's Epistle to the Philippians (*Phil.* ii, 10).

Philistiens, Philistines [late Lat. *Philistinii*], natives of Philistaea whose chief town was Gaza (*Gazan*, above), are referred to in *CT* B *3238 (2048) as unsuccessful defenders of Gaza, *that cité*, in the same line; they are a people of uncertain origin who occupied the south-west part of Palestine.

The form is OFr; cp. ME and mod. English "Philistian", *NED s.v.*

Pycardie, Picardy, old French province including what are now the departments of Somme, parts of Pas-de-Calais, Aisne, and Oise, is mentioned with *Artoys* and *Flaundres* in *CT* A 86 as one of the scenes of the Squire's military activity; see further under *Artoys*.

This regional name, derived from the ethnic name *Picard* "native of Picardy", does not appear until the thirteenth century and is of uncertain origin; see *NED s.v.* "picard", headnote; earlier the Picards were known as *Po(u)hiers*, surviving in the family-name *Pouyer* (Longnon No. 921).

Pileer (of Hercules), the Pillars of Hercules [Lat. *Herculis Columnae*], mentioned in *CT* B *3308 (2118) as set up by Her-

cules, refer in ancient geography to the two promontories between which is the Strait of Gibraltar; one of the two "pillars"
or promontories was Calpe in Hispania Baetica (mod. Rock of
Gibraltar), the other Abyla, a mountain spur on the North
African side of the Strait. As an outlet to the Atlantic the Strait
was thought of as marking one of the "ends" of the earth. On
this and on the suggestion of a similar "pillar" in the East, see
Robinson, pp. 747–48, n. 2117.

Pyze [var. MR VII, 512], Pisa in the Valle del'Arno, 6 m.
from the sea, is mentioned to identify Count Ugolino (*Erl
Hugelyn*) in *CT* B² *3597 (2407), *3599 (2409), *3646 (2456),
and in B² *3606 (2416) and in the preceeding Latin heading to
identify Bishop Ruggieri (*Roger*). In B² 3599 (2409), *3600
(2410) there is a *tour* with *dores* (B² *3615 [2425]), used as a
prison in B² *3600 (2410), *3605 (2415), *3609 (2419), which is
central to the story.

The name looks back to Rom. (Etruscan?) *Pisa* and *Pisae*;
EI XXVII, 392 ff.; Repetti IV, 297 ff.; Matthias 161–62. Chaucer's form is French, the modern English Italian.

Poilleys [var. *Poleyn[e]*, *Pule[y]n*, MR VI, 525], adj. of or
pertaining to Apulia, Apulian (Fr. *pouillois*), a region of SE Italy
famed for its fine horses, is mentioned in *CT* F 195 to describe
a race-horse (*courser*) comparable to one received as a gift by
Cambyus Kan (not formally identifiable with Chinggis Khan);
see also F 193 under *Lumbardye*. In Chaucer's day Apulia
formed part of the Kingdom of Naples.

The Lat. regional name *Apulia*, in medieval times by aphesis
often *Pulia*, looks back to the Samite tribe of the *Apuli*, early
settled in that region. The mod. Fr. descendant of the aphetic

Pulia is *Pouille,* with several OFr derivative adjectives, such as *Puillain* (*Pullan, Polain*), *Puilleis* (*Puilloiz, Pulois*), reflected in the received Chaucer form and in the variants.

Poo [var. MR VI, 248], the Po, largest river of Italy, rises (*CT* E 48) at the foot of Monviso (*Vesulus*) in the Cottian Alps on the French frontier, flows NE and then generally E, ending in a large delta which empties through several mouths into the Adriatic some 35–40 m. S. of Venice, not at or near *Venyse* as Petrarch (B & D 296, 8–10) and Chaucer may imply.

The source of the name is Romano-Celtic *Padus* (Ligurian *Bodincus,* Holder I, 457, Longnon Nos. 25, 1154) of uncertain origin; Holder II, 902–20; *EI* XXVII, 572, Nissen I, 183 ff.; Matthias 162–64.

Poperyng, Poperinghe, *ca* 6 m. from Ypres, West Flanders, Belgium, a town prosperous in the Middle Ages through its cloth manufacture, is mentioned in *CT* B² *1910 (720) as being in *Flaundres* and the birthplace of Sir Thopas.

This *ing*-name appears earliest (877, 1107 A.D.) with the habitative suffix *-hem* in *Pupringa-* (gen. plur.), *Poperinge-hem* "estate or farm of the Puprings or Poperings", the patronymic in turn based on an otherwise unidentified personal name (*OGN* 38, 39). Chaucer's and the modern name show either a loss of the terminal *-hem* or look back to a parallel uncompounded *ing*-name.

Portyngale, Portugal, is mentioned in *CT* B² *4649 (3459) (*With brasile ne with greyn of Portyngale,* without editors' comma after *brasile*) as the exporting country of two dyestuffs, vegetable and insect respectively. For the former see under *brasile,* above.

The insect dye, *greyn*, "dyers' grain" or *Grana tinctorum*, refers to kermes, oldest dyestuff on record (cp. "scarlet" in *Gen.* xxxviii, 28, 30); see further Harold N. and Alma L. Moldenke, *Plants of the Bible* (Waltham, Mass.: Chronica Botanica, 1952), Index, p. 320, col. 1, *s.v.* "Quercus coccifera", also Thompson 111–16 (see *brasile*) and Thompson and Hamilton 46–47, n. 87 (see *brasile*). This blood-red dye was obtained from the dried bodies of the parasite female scale-insect, *coccus ilicis*, after egg-laying and was ignorantly taken in Antiquity to be a seed grain which the dead bodies resemble; these "grains" have also been known as "kermes berries". The insects are found on the leaves of the bushy evergreen shrub or small tree, the *Quercus coccifera*, popularly known as the Kermes oak or Grain oak which flourishes in southern Europe, including Spain and Portugal. See *NED s.v.* "grain", sb.,[1] 10, quotation from 1617 concerning Spaniards and Portuguese as exporters of the same, also *NED s.v.* "kermes" and Du Cange *s.vv.* "graingne", "1 grana", and "2 granum". On the kermes oak in England, see W. J. Bean, 'Quercus coccifera', *The Gardener's Chronicle*, LXV (April 19th 1916), 195, with photograph, also Alfred Rehder, *Manual of Cultivated Trees and Shrubs* (2d ed., New York, 1940), p. 162. Chaucer may have become familiar with the source of both brazil-wood and kermes, as well as of other commodities, through his office of Controller of Customs which he held in one way or another between 1374 and 1386. *Greyn* is used here along with *brasile* to suggest the high complexion of the Nun's Priest, as it is in *CT* B² *1917 (727) with reference to Sir Thopas' coloring; for a figurative use applied to *colours* in the sense of "figures of speech" see *CT* F 511.

The name (OFr *Portingale*, also *Portegale*), obsolete by-form of the name Portugal (see *NED s.v.*), looks back to Rom. *Portus*

Cales (Holder I, 695, "Cales" 2), site of Oporto, today surviving in the name Vila Nova de Gaya on the left bank of the Douro (Span. Duero), Portugal.

Pru[y]ce [var. Skeat I, 312, n. *ad loc.*; MR V, 6]:

I. sb. Prussia (Germ. *Preussen*, Fr. *Prusse*) in Chaucer's day designated essentially a part of the Baltic litoral east of Pomerania and the Vistula, more or less equivalent to later East Prussia, first with Marienburg, later Königsberg as the seat of the rule of the Teutonic Knights. The population was to all intents and purposes Christian and largely German, and the rule of the Teutonic Knights of the Order of the Sword was beginning to weaken. *Pruyse* is mentioned in *BD* 1025 as a remote place to which the Duchess of Lancaster would not have sent an admirer on an irksome or futile mission (cp. *Alysaundre*, *Carre Nar*, *Drye See*, *Tartarye* I, *Turkye*, *Walakye*). In *CT* A 53 it is mentioned as a region where the Knight on an expedition or sojourn, presumably with the Teutonic Knights, sat at the head of the table in precedence over *alle nacions*, where "nations" refer to national groupments quite likely at the Table of Honor; see A. S. Cook, 'Beginning the Board in Prussia', *Journal of English and Germanic Philology*, XIV (1915), 375–88, also Cook 209–12.

II. *Pruce* (var. MR V, 204), adj. of or pertaining to Prussia, Prussian, is used in *CT* A 2122 to describe a type of shield carried by some of Palamon's adherents. The adjective is identical with the substantive, I, above.

The ethnic name seems first to be recorded as *Prusi* "Prussians" in the *Russian Primary Chronicle*, Foreword, § 4 (C & S–W) and is the name of a Baltic tribe closely related to the Lithuanians (see *Lettow*). Early latinized *Pruzzi*, it appears as OFr

Pru(y)ce, whence Chaucer's form; see *NED s.v.* "Prussian",
B, sb. headnote. The variants *Sprus, Spruce, Sprewse*, though
probably not Chaucer's, are frequent in the manuscripts and
in a sense legitimate in that such forms (Med. Lat. *Sprucia*)
are common in the Middle Ages and long after and the source
of the common English tree-name (*NED s.v.* "spruce").

R

Ravenne, Ravenna [Lat. *Ravenna*], in antiquity a sea-port
of Gallia Transpadana, now chief city of the prov. of Ravenna,
Italy, was in Boethius' day the chief city of Theoderic the
Ostrogoth (in later legend his chief city came to be Verona
[*Berne*]); in *Bo* 1, pr. 4, l. 136 (130–35) it is a *cité* and is men-
tioned as a place from which Boethius' adversaries Opulio and
Gaudentius fled.

Chaucer's form is OFr.

[The] Rede See, the Red Sea [Lat. *Mare Rubrum*], the narrow
sea separating the coast of Arabia and Egypt, is mentioned in
Bo 3, m. 3, l. 6 (685–90) as a source of precious stones; in *CT*
B 490 it is alluded to as *see* with reference to *Exod.* xiii–xiv.

Reynes, Rennes [dép. Ille-et-Vilaine] at the confluence of
the Ille and the Vilaine and in ancient times known as *Condatē* "confluence" (Longnon Nos. 127–35), is used in *BD* 255
to define *cloth* with reference to a kind of fine linen or lawn made
in the town; see *NED s.v.* "raines" for many references. Cp.
chalon and *Tars* for other town-names identifying textiles.

The name, replacing older *Condatē* (Holder I, 1092–95 "Con-
dati-" § 9), looks back to the Gaulish tribal name *Rēdones*,

perhaps meaning "swift ones" or "chariot using people"; see Holder II, 1102–05, Gröhler I, 80. Chaucer's *Reynes* reflects OFr *Raynes*, by-form of Rennes.

[The] Rochele, La Rochelle (dép. Charente-Inférieure), France, capital of the old province of Aunis and in 1360–72 an English possession, was in the fourteenth century an almost independent commune; it is mentioned in *CT* C 571 along with *Burdeux* as an importing source of French wines.

The name is made up of **rocca* "rock" of unknown origin (Holder II, 1200; Gröhler II, 92–93; M–L No. 7357) plus the diminutive suffix *-elle* (Gröhler II, 94), the rock in question probably referring to some small stone fortification early built as a customs barrier or the like (Longnon No. 2224). In the tenth century the name appears translated as Lat. *Rupella* where Lat. *rupis* 'rock' substitutes for *rocca* (Longnon 2218).

Rodopeya, -peye, a mountain range in Thrace, now the Despoto Dagh (Lat. *Rhodope, -es*), is in the Legend of Phyllis obviously thought of as a region and city (*lond*, *LGW* 2423, 2427, 2434) where Demophon rests up (l. 2437) after an arduous sea-voyage from Troy; later, when able to walk again, he proceeds to the court (l. 2440), presumably in the city of *Rodopeya*. The queen of the country (l. 2424) is *Phillis*, in l. 2498 of *Rodopeye*.

The form *Rodopeye*, Latinized as *Rodopeya*, is based on the Lat. adj.-type *Rhodopeius* "a Rhodopeian", poetically used for "Thracian".

Roman [Romeyn], adj. and sb.

A. adj. pertaining to Rome, ancient and medieval (cp *Rome*, below) and its inhabitants: *CT* B 954, *3526 (2336) (defining

Galien), *LGW* 1812. Stories of ancient Rome are referred to loosely as (*olde*) *Romayn gestes* in *CT* B 1126, E 2284.

B. sb. sing. and pl., an inhabitant of Rome, ancient and medieval: (1) in sing. in *BD* 1084 (defining Livy), *CT* D 647 (defining P. Sempronius Sophus), F 1404, *Bo* 2, pr. 7, l. 79 (545–50); (2) in the plur. in *CT* B 291, 394, *2178 (988), *2629 (1439), *3551 (2361) (defining Aurelian), B*4555 (3365), F 1401, G 121, *LGW* G 275, 627, 630, 1695, 1812.

Chaucer's forms are based on Lat. *Rōmānus* and OFr *romein*, respectively.

Rome [Lat. *Rōma*]. A. Rome of classical antiquity, cut through by the river Tiber (*Tybre*, below), is mentioned as the center or symbol of the Roman kingdom, republic or empire, or as early Christian Rome in *CT* B *3866 (2676); *BD* 1063; *LGW* 584, 595, 1710, 1712; *Bo* 2, pr. 7, l. 72 (540–45). *Rome* identifies or defines kings of ancient Rome (*LGW* 1680–81), consuls (*Bo* 2, pr. 2, l. 72 [310–15]; 3, pr. 4, l. 13 [690–95]), Julius Caesar (*CT* B *3867 [2677]), "*lordes*" (Caesar and Pompey, *Astr* Pt. i, § 10, ll. 9–11 [45–50]), Pompey (*CT* B*3879 [2689]), and the late emperor Claudius II (*CT* B *3525 [2335]). The Roman commonwealth is the *commune of R.* (*Bo* 2, pr. 7, l. 68 [540–45]) and the praetorship the *provostrye of R.* (*Bo* 3, pr. 4, l. 90 [710–75]). It is referred to as *cité of R.* in *Bo* 2, pr. 6, ll. 18–19 (485–90) and *Bo* 2, m. 6, l. 4 (515–20) and in *CT* B *4560–61 (3370–71); *toun of R.* in *LGW* 586, 591, 1861; *CT* G 361; *Rome toun* in *LGW* F 257 (G 211), 1691, 1869. The poss. sg. *Romes* (*HF* 1504 [3, 414]) refers to the glorious past that was Rome's, the Lat. gen. sg. *Rome* (= *Rōmae*) to Lucretia (*LGW* Legend of Lucrece, head and end). It is referred to merely as *toun* in *CT* G 173, *LGW* 1727, 1867, and implicitly in *CT* C

118 (here cp. Gower, *CA* vii, 5131: *at Rome*). Rome and the surrounding region, the Roman Campagna is implied in *lond* and *regioun* in *CT* C 113, 122. In *CT* G 975 it is a symbol of greatness.

The Capitol (*Capitolie*, Lat. *Capitolium*) is mentioned in *CT* B*3893 (2703), *3895 (2705); the Appian Way (Lat. *Via Appia*), as if a place, in *CT* G 172; the Catacombs (*Seintes Buryeles*) in G 186, referred to as a *place* in G 183; the cathedral church of St Cecilia in Trastevere (*Chirche of Seint Cecilie*) mentioned in G 550, is said to have been built on the site of the house of Valerian and Cecilia (G 514, 550, and implicitly in G 141–42, 218–19). The house of Lucius Tarquinius Collatinus and Lucretia is mentioned in *LGW* 1713, 1716, 1778, and described *passim*; according to more orthodox tradition it was in the Sabine town of Collatia near Rome.

B. The Rome of Boethius (*ca* 475–525) during the reign of Theoderic the Ostrogoth is mentioned in *Bo* 1, pr. 4, l. 189 (145–50), *Bo* 2, pr. 7, l. 80 (540–50); in *Bo* 1, pr. 4, l. 265 (160–65) it is the *cité of R.*, and in *Bo* 1, pr. 4, ll. 102–11 (120–25) it defines two contemporary consuls.

In the *Man of Law's Tale*, placed in the following century, it defines a *strete* (*CT* B 1103) and the lodgings (*in*) of Ælla, first king of Deira (later part of Northumbria, England), *regn.* 560–588 A.D.

C. Medieval Rome, often thought of as a pilgrimage center and the seat of the Papal Court is mentioned in *HF* 1930 (3, 840); *RR* 1093; *CT* F 231; in *CT* B 156, 309 it defines a late sixth-century emperor. It is the *toun of R.* in *CT* B 1148 and is referred to merely as *toun* in B 310. It is the goal of pilgrims in *TC* 2, 36; *Astr* Pref. l. 47 (5–11), and in *CT* A 465 and B 995 it is *Rome toun*. It is identified with the Papal Court in *RR*

7190 (cp. l. 7198); *CT* A 671, 687, E 737, and implicitly in B 991 (cp. l. 992).

Chaucer's form is based on OFr.

Romeyn, see **Roman.**

Rouchestre, Rochester (K), across the Medway from Strood and immediately contiguous to Chatham and Gillingham and 30 m. from *Southwerk* on the *Caunterbury Wey* (*q.v.*), is mentioned in *CT* B *3119 (1926) as a point near which the pilgrims are at the beginning of the Monk's Tale. Muirhead *England* 17–21. Rochester was well-known as an overnight stopping place between Southwark and Canterbury, indeed the only other suitable place apart from Dartford [*Derteford*] and Ospringe [*Ospringe*]. See Furnivall 22, Littlehales 25, Tatlock 483–84, who is almost alone in rejecting Rochester as a conjectural overnight stop.

In all *CT* manuscripts fragment B² [VII] is separated from B¹ [II] with the result that mention of Rochester follows that of *Sidyngborne*, itself some 11 m. nearer Canterbury. This discrepancy, ignored by the early editors, was noted by Henry Bradley who in turn pointed it out to Furnivall (p. 22) who adjusted the order of tales to take care of this point and was followed by many other scholars (Pratt 1143 for list). MR and Robinson have unfortunately reverted to the Ms., particularly Ellesmere, arrangement and this again has led to all manner of discussion. Robinson (889, col. 1 *ad fin.*) excuses or justifies the manuscript arrangement as one among "so many small discrepancies" and to be viewed as a "slip of Chaucer's own"; to Lawrence 102 "it seems less like a slip than a somersault". If it represents a slip on Chaucer's part (as it surely is not) but the result of an arrangement bungled by scribes (as it surely is), this should earn Chaucer a place high in the *New Yorker* magazine's department of "Our Forgetful Authors". See further Lawrence 116–18, Pratt 1159–61 with full literature.

The name looks back to OE *Hrofes-ćeaster* as if meaning "the Roman fort of one *Hrof*". For the rather elaborate development of a personal name *Hrof* from Romano-British *Durobrivae*, apparently assumed by the Anglo-Saxons, see *DEPN s.v.*

Rouncival, see [**Westminster, city of**].

Ruce, Russye, formally Russia, though by no means answering to the present-day Soviet Union or the former Russian Empire, is used by Chaucer in two connections. In *CT* A 54 *Ruce* is mentioned along with *Lettow* as an area where the Knight had been on military expeditions and would correspond perhaps to Russian territory eastward toward, say, Smolensk on the Dneiper, at that time near the border of the great kingdom of Lithuania (*Lettow*). In *CT* F 10 *Russeye* is a land said to have been warred upon by Cambyus Kan (not formally identifiable with Chinggis Khan), *Tartre* king of the Golden Horde with his capital then at *Sarray*.

The origin of the name, earlier *Rus*, is not altogether certain but may well look back to a name-type *Ruotsi*, earlier *Rootsi*, Finnish name of Sweden, perhaps extended to cover Russian territory under Swedish (Varangian) control. By Chaucer's time the name had long since, however, lost any Scandinavian connotation; see further C & S–W.

Med. Lat. *Russia* (whence mod. Engl. Russia) parallels OFr *Ro(u)s(s)ie*, whence Chaucer's *Russye*; his *Ruce* seems to answer to an adjective form corresponding to Fr. *russe* and Engl. *russ* (cp. *NED s.v.*).

S

Sayne [Seyne] [var. *Spayne*, MR VI, 629, and *mount* for *mouth*], great river of northern France, passes through Paris and Rouen and enters the English Channel between Honfleur and Le Havre (since 1516) (dép. Seine-Inférieure). The estuary (*mouth of Sayne*) is mentioned in *CT* F 1222 as the northern limit, of which the *Gerounde* is the southern, of a stretch of the French coast to be cleared of rocks and reefs dangerous to shipping. In *RR* 118 (*Roman de la Rose* 112) a stream in the Garden of the Rose is said to be somewhat smaller than the *Sayne*.

The name looks back to a Ligurian(?) *Sēquana*, whence the OFr, Chaucer's and the modern forms; adopted into OHG as *Sîgana* (with substitution of Germanic *î* for Gaulish *ē*) it yielded *inter alia* OE *Sîʒen*; Holder II, 1505–10; Gröhler, I, 13–14; Förster *Themse* 582. The variant *mount of Spayne* for *mouth of Sayne* recalls *HF* 1116–17 (3, 26–27).

Saluce[s] [var. MR VII, 247, 249, 290, 291], Saluzzo (prov. Cuneo), region and town in *Pemond* near the *Poo* and 31 m. SSW of Turin, was before and after Chaucer's day the center of a marquisate, of which the first marquis was Bonigacio del Vaste (d. 1135); see *EI* XXX, 570–73. It is mentioned alone in *CT* E 420, 753, 775; in E 414, 1005 it is a *toun*, in E 1005 a *cité*. It is thought of as a district or *contré* in E 44, 63 (*noble*), 75, 435, 615 and in E 64 is *that lond*. The fictional first marquis is here Walter (Gualtieri) who in E 772 is the *Markys of Saluce*, in E 64, 91, 92 and frequently *passim* simply *markys*; Griselde is the marchioness, in E 394 the *newe markysesse*, the same designation being in a sense transferred to her daughter in E 942, 1014.

In the town is the marquis' *paleys* (E 197, 262, 389, 875) or *hous* (E 478, 820, 956, 973) with a *halle* (E 263, 980, 1029, 1119), *chambre(s)* (E 263, 961, 980), and *houses of office* "servants' quarters and utility buildings" (*NED s.v.* "house" sb.,[1] 14; "office" sb. 9, and cp. "office-house"). Griselde's bedroom (*chambre*) is mentioned in E 515, 525, 1115, Walter's in E 870. Not far out in the country is a charming village (*throop*, E 199, 208; *village*, E 200, 272) with a village-well (E 276), the home of Janicula/Janicle (Giannùcolo), Griselde's father (E 277, 284; *hous*, E 332, 809, 871, 896; *place*, E 862); a front *dore* is mentioned in E 367, a *chambre* in E 324, 330.

The name is first recorded in the eleventh century; see *EI* XXX, 571–72 (for history), 572–73 (on the marquisate). Petrarch latinized the name of the region as *terra Saluciarum* (B & D 296, 15); Chaucer's form is French.

Samaritan, sb. a Samaritan [late Lat. *Samaritanus*], a native or inhabitant of Samaria, a district of Palestine (Lat. *Samaritis*), named for its chief town, anciently the capital of the kingdom of Israel, is used in *CT* D 16, 22, specifically of the woman of Samaria (*John* iv, 7-18).

Chaucer's form is a learned adaptation of the Lat. adj.

Sarray, Saraï Berké or New Saraï, once great trading center and in Chaucer's day (since Uzbek Khan 1312–40) capital of the Khanate of the Golden Horde on the Akhtuba branch of the Lower Volga in the Stalingrad (formerly Tsaritsyn) region, was predominantly Turkish with not many Mongol residents; it was destroyed in 1395 by the Berla chieftain Timūr i leng (Persian) "Timur the Lame", Turk. Tämür Läng, whence the western form Tamerlane, Christopher Marlowe's *Tambur-*

laine the Great (G & I 139–40); see *E Isl* IV,[1] 158–59; G & I
70–71, 75, 135–47. It is mentioned in *CT* F 9 as a place in the
(*land of*) *Tartarye* II, and in F 46 is said to be a city of Cambyus
Kan (not answering formally to Chinggis Khan), throughout
which he had his birthday proclaimed and sumptuously celebrated. This New Saraï (Berké) is opposed to Saraï Batu or
Old Saraï in the Volga delta (G & I 70–71, 73).

The Khan's palace (G & I 136) is mentioned in F 60, with
a *halle* (F 86, 92), *halle-dore* (F 80), and *deys* (F 59). There is a
keep or donjon ([*heighe*] *tour*, F 76, 340) where some of the
magical birthday presents were stored for safe-keeping; the idea
of the *tour* may reflect the Tower of London (see *London*).
There is also a *temple*, in the case of the Lower Volga Moslem
Tatars a mosque (G & I 81, 137, 154), where the assembled
company worships (F 296–93). Another richly tapestried room
is the *chambre of parementz* (F 296) in which there is music,
dancing, and feasting. Somewhere outside is a *park* (F 391)
with a walk (*trench*) cut through the trees or shrubbery (F 391),
the scene of the action of Part ii of the unfinished poem.

The name (and word) *Sarray*, i.e., Saraï, is Turkish, adapted
from Persian *sarai* "palace"; see *NED s.v.* "serai[1]".

Satalye, Antalya, formerly Adalia [Lat. *Attalia* in Pamphilia,
Med. Lat. *Satalia*], vilayet of Konya (ancient *Iconium*), Turkey
in Asia, seaport at the head of the Gulf of Antalya W of the
Gulf of Iskenderun, formerly Alexandretta, was in Chaucer's
day in the hands of the Seljuk Turks and their chief city (*E Isl* I,
126–27; Cook 230–31). It is mentioned in *CT* A 58 as a place
in the Levant (cp. *Lyeys*, *Palatye*) where the Knight was active
in some of Pierre de Lusignan's campaigns (Cook 231–32).

The name looks back to ancient *Attalia*, one of several Asia

Minor cities named after Attalus II (B.C. 200–138), king of
Pergamum; the town is mentioned in *Acts* xiv, 25, as the port
from which SS Paul and Barnabas set sail for Antioch (v, 26).
The Med. Lat. *Satalia* shows a prosthetic *S-* resulting from a
false division of a preceding Greek preposition *eis* "to"; for
this and other examples of the same phenomenon, see W. B.
Sedgwick, *Rev. of Eng. Stud.*, II (1926), 346.

Scithia, Cithe, Cithia, formally the land of the Scythians
[Lat. *Scytha, -ae* m., *Scythes, -ae,* m., mostly in the plural],
Scythia, was among the ancients a vaguely and fluctuatingly
defined region, at times at least, roughly corresponding to the
Russian steppe between the Carpathian mountains and the
river Don. Whatever notions Chaucer may have had about the
geography—and vague indeed they must have been—his use
of the name obviously derives from Statius' *Thebaid* XII, 519 ff.,
where Scythia is associated with Lake Maeotis (l. 527), now
the Sea of Azov. For Chaucer Scythia was identical with his
Femenye (above), the land of the Amazons in NE Turkey. The
geography makes utter nonsense.

The country is referred to as *Scithia* in *CT* A 867 and in A
882 and *Anel* 36–37 (*Cithia*) defines the the queen, Hippolyta.
The Scythians, i.e., Amazons, are described as the *aspre folk
of Cithe* in *Anel* 23, based on *Thebaid* XII, 519–20.

The forms (*S*)*cithia* are Latin, while *Cithe* (mod. Fr. *Scythie*)
is OFr.

Scotland, Scotland, is mentioned in *CT* B 718 [var. MR V,
507] as a region toward which (*to-Scotland-ward*) King Ælla of
"*Northumberlond*" proceeded to attack his enemies.

The name looks back to OE *Scot-land* (pron. *shot-land*) "land of the Irish who settled Scotland, of Gaels"; see *Scottes*, below. The later pronunciation *skot-* is presumably due to Scandinavian influence; cp. *Engelond*, above.

Scottes, Scotsmen, natives of Scotland, are mentioned in *CT* B 580 as enemies of *"Northumberlond"* against whom Ælla's Constable was to hold the royal castle.

The name looks back to OE *Scot*, plur. *Scottas*, meaning originally "Irishman", later by extension to the Irish settlers in *Scotland* (*q.v.* above). On the etymology see *NED s.v.* sb. 1.

[Sea of Galilee], is referred to as the *see* in *CT* A 698 in connection with the miracle of St Peter's walking over its waters to Jesus (*Matth.* xiv, 29). See further *Galilee*, above.

Seyne, see **Sayne.**

Seint-Denys, Saint-Denis-sur-Seine (dép. Seine), France, suburb of Paris and 8 m. N of the city on route 6, is famous for its once powerful abbey, founded by Dagobert I (d. 638 A.D.) and rebuilt in the twelfth and thirteenth centuries; it is mentioned in *CT* B²*1191 (21), *1249 (59), *1257 (67), *1498 (308), *1516 (326) as the home of a wealthy banker-merchant. The saint himself is mentioned in B²*1341 (151) and often elsewhere in Chaucer.

Ancient *Catulliacus* (*fundus*) was renamed for St Dionysius (Denis) (*Sancti Dionysii basilica*), legendary first bishop of Paris; of the many localities similarly named after that saint the present town is the most famous; Holder I, 849–50; Gröhler II, 402; Longnon No. 1693.

Seint-Jame [var. MR V, 42; cp. var. *Seint-Jakes*], Santiago
(de Compostela, also de Galicia), prov. of Coruña, in the old
province of *Galice* in NW Spain, is mentioned in *CT* A 466
as the scene of one of the Wife's many pilgrimages. In Chaucer's
day Santiago was one of the principal pilgrim resorts of the
West, still today a great tourist center, especially for Spaniards.
The saint himself is often invoked and quoted elsewhere in
Chaucer.

Chaucer's *Seint-Jame*, based on the name of St James the
Apostle who supposedly preached in Galicia and whose bones
were reputedly discovered at Compostela, is in effect an OFr
translation of Span. *Sant-iago*, where *Iago* is a dialectal (Gali-
cian?) form of *Jacobo*, *Jaime* "James". OFr *Saint-Jame* is in
turn a variant of *Saint-Jacques* (cp. var. above) (see *NED s.v.*
"James"). This *Iago* is presumably identical with the Iago of
Shakespeare's *Othello* (both names are trisyllabic). *Compostela*,
site of this great shrine, is very likely a diminutive of Span.
composta "fortification" (*EUI* LIV, 247). Unlikely and no doubt
reflecting popular etymologizing are derivations on the order
of *campus stella* from a star said to have shown where the saint's
remains were (*EI* XXX, 786).

Septe [var. MR V, 529] is mentioned in *CT* B 947 along with
Jubaltare to define the limits of the 15 m. strait (*narwe mouth*,
B 946) known to Chaucer as the Strait of *Marrok*, today the
Strait of Gibraltar (*Jubaltare*). *Septe* refers to the ridge with
seven peaks in former Spanish Morocco (administratively in
the prov. of Cadiz), called in antiquity *Septem Fratres* from their
"fraternal" appearance; specifically in question is the highest
(636 ft) peak of the ridge, *Abyla* of antiquity, today Span.
Monte del Hacho "beacon-hill mountain", Fr. *Montagne des*

Singes (cp. the Gibraltar apes) and it is surely this, not the little seaport of Ceuta (today of consequence as an oil-bunkering station), that Chaucer had in mind. Together, *Abyla* and *Calpe* (Gibraltar) formed the *Herculis Columnae* or Pillars of Hercules of antiquity (see *Pileer*).

At the foot of the ridge was early a Carthaginian colony, probably called *Exilissa* or *Lissa civitas*, later *civitas ad Septem Fratres*, early reduced to *Septon*, later *Sebta* (whence Arab. *Sabta*), in turn with vocalization of the *b* yielding modern *Ceuta* as the name of the town, but not of the promontory. See *EUI* I, 433 "Abila"; XII, 1514 "Ceuta"; XXXII, 1264 "Marabut (al-)"; *E Isl* I, 836–38; *EB* V, 176.

Sereyens, sb. pl. Chinese [Lat. *Seres, -um*], whose *contré* is mentioned in *Bo* 2, m. 5, l. 12 (475–80) as a source of fine wool (*bryhte* ["clean, white"] *fleeses*).

Chaucer's form has almost certainly been influenced (by misunderstanding?) with "Syrian"; cp. *Syrien*, below.

Sheene is the early name of Richmond (Sr), residence of English kings from Edward I (*regn.* 1272–1307) to 1394, when Richard II had the palace at least partially razed; in 1499 what remained was destroyed by fire but was magnificently rebuilt by Henry VII, who changed the name of the manor to Richmond in honor of his own title of Earl of Richmond inherited from his father Edmund Tudor and based on Richmond on the Swale (YNR). Muirhead *London* 482–83. It is mentioned in *LGW* Pr F 497 (omitted in G) as an alternative royal palace to *Eltham* (*q.v.*) where Chaucer might deliver the completed *Legend of Good Women* to Richard II's first queen, Anne of Bohemia (died June 7th, 1394).

The name looks back to some form or derivative of OE *sciene* "fair, beautiful" and presumably meant "the beautiful spot or site". *PN* XI *Sr* 1, 26, 65–66. The name survives in the adjoining Sheen Common and in the village of East Sheen (S.W.18) (in contrast to West Sheen or Richmond).

Sheffeld, Sheffield [YWR] at the confluence of the Sheaf with the Don, since the present reference famous for its cutlery, is mentioned in *CT* A 3933 (var. MR V, 390) to define a knife ("*thwitel*") carried by the miller Symond or Simkin. Muirhead *England* 432–35.

The name looks back to the river-name Sheaf (OE **scéaþ*, *scǽþ* "boundary") and originally applied to the region or *feld* on the river. See *ERN* 360–61.

Sidyngborne, Sittingbourne (K) on the Swale, 39 m. from London and adjoined on the N by the ancient borough of Milton Regis or Royal on the Swale (*Middel-tún* of the *Anglo-Saxon Chronicle s.a.* 893, 897, 964), is mentioned in *CT* D 847 (var. MR VI, 84) as the place before reaching which the Summoner will have told a tale about friars. Muirhead *England* 22.

The name looks back to OE *Sídinga-burna*, m., or *-burne*, f., "stream of the hillside-dwellers(?)", with reference to the Swale. *DEPN s.v.*

Symois, the Simois [Lat. *Simois*], mod. Turk. Dümberek su, a small river in the Troad, tributary of the ancient Scamander, mod. Medere cayı, which flows into the Dardanelles, is in *TC* 4, 1548, incorrectly said to cut through Troy.

Chaucer's form is Latin.

Synay, Mt Sinai (in the Bible alternately but less commonly known as Horeb or Oreb), the mountain which gives its name to the Sinaitic peninsula, projecting into the Red Sea between the Gulf of Suez and the Gulf of Akaba, is in *CT* D 1887 a *mountaigne* (var. *mount*) and is mentioned in connection with Moses' fast of forty days and forty nights (*Exod.* xxxiv 28). See also *Oreb*, above.

Syrien, adj. Chinese (or Syrian?) is used in *Bo* 2, m. 5, l. 14 (475–80) to define a *contré*, a land producing white wool (*white fleeses*). See *Seryens*, above, and *Surryen*, below.

Sysile, the island of Sicily [Lat. *Sicilia*], originally a settlement of the Ligurian tribe of the Siculi, driven from their home on the Tiber (*Tybre*, below), is mentioned in *Bo* 3, pr. 5, l. 26 (725–30) in connection with the well-known story of Dionysius the Elder, tyrant of Syracuse, and the so-called sword of Damocles (ll. 28–30).

Chaucer's form is OFr (mod. Fr. *la Sicile*).

Soler Halle, conceivably but with no certainty to be identified with the former King's Hall, Cambridge, originally the handsome timbered house of one Robert de Croyland situated between the present Great Gate, Trinity Chapel and the sundial and leased by Edward II in 1317 as a hostel or student rooming-house for his "King's Scholars or Childer". If *Soler Halle* does refer to the King's Hall, this seems to be the only instance of its being so referred to. Twenty years later it was bought outright by Edward III for the same purpose; the building—gradually other buildings were bought in and added—remained a hostel or "hall", not a college in the modern sense of the word for a couple of centuries. On the "hall' vs the "college" system in the early English universities, see H. S. Salter, *Medieval Oxford* (Oxford, 1936), pp. 102–03; note that Trinity Hall is the only college that keeps the name of "Hall". In Chaucer's day King's Hall may have housed some twenty students. In 1546 Henry VIII bought up King's Hall and the neighboring Michaelhouse and Physwick's Hostel to form the present Trinity College. See George M. Trevelyan, *Trinity College: An Historical Sketch* (Cambridge, 1943), pp. 1–11 ("Proto-Trinity"), with map of the old arrangements p. 2.

Soler Halle, which, had it survived as an academic entity, would today be written Sollar Hall, is mentioned in *CT* A 3990 (var. MR V, 395) as being at Cambridge (*Cantebregge*), in A 3989 it is a "*greet collegge*", i.e., a large academic building or complex of buildings (*NED* "college", 5); in A 4003 it is a *halle*. The young teen-age boys are looked after by a "*Wardeyn*" (A 3999, 4005, 4006, 4112). There was also a purchasing agent or manciple (A 3993, 4029).

The element *soler* (*NED* "sollar") referred to the upper chambers of Robert de Croyland's house (if the identification with King's Hall is right) above the main downstairs rooms (OE *solor*, OFr *soler*, *solair*, adapted from Lat. *solarium*).

Southwerk, Southwark (Sr), now a metropolitan borough of London (S.E.1) stretching along the S bank of the Thames between Blackfriars and London Bridge, was even in the fourteenth century virtually a part of London proper; it was annexed to the city in 1549 (Darby 363). It is the starting point of Chaucer's Canterbury pilgrimage and is mentioned as such in *CT* A 20, 718; in A 3140 it defines the local ale; in A 566 it is referred to as a *toun*. Two inns out of probably several or many are re-

ported being there. The *Tabard* (A 20, 719), run by the historically identified Henry (Harry) Bailey and named from the
short sleeveless jacket used as the inn-sign, was an actual hostelry
of that day (Manly 498; Robinson 651, n. 20; Bowden 38–39)
and stood on the east side of Borough High St; here at one time
or another have stood a series of famous inns including Shakespeare's "White Hart" (2 *H VI*, iv, 8). The present Talbot
Yard in the Borough High St is on the site of the old Tabard.
Muirhead *London* 318–319. In A 23 it is a *hostelrye* with spacious
stables (*stables wyde*, A 28), a *herberwe* or lodging place (*NED*
"harboury") in A 765, and in A 800 a *place*. The name is adapted
from Old French *tabart* of uncertain origin. Another inn, the
Belle (*CT* A 719) is also mentioned, not certainly identified but
perhaps across the road from the Tabard (Robinson 668, n. 719).

The name *Southwerk* looks back to OE *súþ* "south" and
ȝeweorc "fortification", thus the "southern fortification" with
reference to its position on the S bank of the Thames, or perhaps
"fortification of the people of Surrey". See *PN* XI *Sr* 29–31.

Spayne [var. MR VII, 66], Spain (Span. *España*, Fr. *Espagne*), is mentioned in *HF* 1117 (3, 27) with reference to a
mountain peak, possibly *Jubaltare* (see *Hous of Fame*); in *CT*
A 409 perhaps with reference to the entire Atlantic coast of
the Iberian peninsula, including Portugal; in B² *3565 (2375) it
defines Pedro, king of Leon and Castile (1350–69), and in
C 565, 570 the heady wine of *Lepe*.

The following Spanish localities are mentioned: *Algezir,
Aragon, Cataloigne, Fynystere, Galice, Gernade, Jubaltare, Lepe,
Seint-Jame, Septe* in Africa, also indirectly Cordoba (*corde-
wane*) and Toledo (*Tolletanes*).

The name looks back with aphesis to Lat. *Hispania* (*Ispannie,*

above). Chaucer's form is OFr *Spaigne*, var. *Espaigne*, whence
Fr. *Espagne*.

Stix, lit. the Styx, river of the Greek underworld [Lat. *Styx*,
-yges, *-ygos*] by which the gods swore, is in *TC* 4, 1540 *the put*
("pit") *of helle* and viewed as a place of torment, perhaps meant
for Hades as a whole; on this medieval conception of the Styx
see Spencer, *Speculum*, II (1927), 180–181.
    Chaucer's form is Latin.

[**Strait of Gibraltar**], see *Strayte* under *Marrok* and *narwe
mouth* under *Jubaltare* and *Septe*, also *Pileer*.

Stratford-atte-Bowe, Bow, E.13, formerly Stratford at Bow
or le Bow (OFr *le* = *lez* "near, by" [Lat. *latus*]), about 3 m.
E of St Paul's, is in Middlesex county in the metropolitan
borough of Poplar in the notorious Limehouse district. It is
mentioned in *CT* A 127 to define the Anglo-French or Hainaut(?)
type French of the Prioress, Madame Eglentyne, probably
though not absolutely necessarily a member of the Benedictine
nunnery of St Leonard's (Manly 504–05; Bowden 94, 101–02).
It is also quite likely that Chaucer had this same religious foundation in mind in *HF* 116–17 when he humorously speaks of
making a two-mile pilgrimage to the *Corseynt Leonard*; see
H. M. Smyser, 'Chaucer's Two-mile Pilgrimage', *Mod. Lang.
Notes*, LVI (1941), 206–07.
    Like all "stratfords" the name looks back to OE *strǽte* "high-
way" and *ford* "ford" to describe a place where a main road
crosses a stream, here a branch of the Lea. The element *Bow(e)*
(OE *boga* m. "bow") describes the arched bridge said to have
been built in the time of Henry I (*regn.* 1100–35); for a discussion

of the lore connected with the building of the bridge see *PN*
XVIII *Mx* 134.

Strother is said in *CT* A 4014 to be the name of the *toun*
in which Alain and John, student residents of *Soler Halle*,
were born; it is said to be *fer in the north, I cannot telle wher*
(A 4015). Today this is a lost name but a Strother family, surely
taking its name from the town or district, has long been associated with, and prominent in, Northumberland. In the fourteenth
century there was a Castle Strother in Glendale in Wooler and
an Alan and John Strother were prominent (Manly 561, n.
4014); in the seventeenth century there was the medical writer
Edward Strother born in Alnwick (*DNB* XIX, 62–63).
  The name almost surely looks back to OE*stróðor, a derivative
of OE *stróp, stród* "marshy land overgrown with brushwood";
cp. Strood (K) under *Rouchestre*, and see *DEPN* "*stród*" with
the statement that "*strother*" "is also found in pl. ns" but without any instances being cited.

Surrye, Syria [Lat. *Syria*, also *Siria*, *Suria*], a land in SW
Asia Minor on the Mediterranean, under Graeco-Roman ad-
ministration essentially the valley of the Orintes, and corresponding territorially at least in part to that northern part of
the United Arab Republic of the same name, is mentioned in
CT B 134, 173, 177, 279, 387, 441, 955, 1108 as of the late sixth
century; in B 177 *et passim* it is ruled by a Mohamedan sultan
(*sowdan*).
  Chaucer's form is OFr.

Surryen [-ien], adj. and sb. a Syrian, native or inhabitant of
Syria (*Surrye*, above).

A. In *CT* B *3529 (2339) it is used of Syrians of the third century A.D. as one of a number of peoples who did not dare face Queen Zenobia of Palmyra (*Palymerie*, above) in battle.

B. In *CT* B 394, 435, 963 it is used of sixth-century Syrians of the time of Ælla, first king of Deira (later part of Northumbria, England), *regn.* 560–88; in B 153 it is used adjectivally.

Chaucer's form is OFr (mod. *syrien*), looking back to a late Lat. *Syrianus.

T

Tagus, the Tagus [Lat. *Tagus*, Span. *Tajo*, Port. *Tejo*], largest river of the Iberian peninsula, rises in Mt Muela de San Juan in Spain and, flowing past Toledo, forms the boundary between Spain and Portugal and empties into the Bay of Lisbon. In *Bo* 3, m. 10. l. 13 (960–65) it is mentioned, along with the *Hermus* (above) and *Indus* (above), as a river noted for its gold-yielding gravel (*goldene gravelis*).

Chaucer's form is Latin.

Tars [var. MR V, 207–08] is used in *CT* A 2160 to define a textile worn in ancient Athens by King Emetreus of India and, though often used alone to refer to some kind of fine silk favored in the fourteenth and fifteenth centuries (*NED s.v.* "tars"), it is, like "raines" (see *Reynes*), all but certainly based on a place-name. The name in question is very likely the Cilician seaport of Tarsus, birthplace of St Paul, on the now silted-up Cydnus; in Chaucer's day it was in the kingdom of Lesser Armenia (*Armenia Minor*). Turkish since the sixteenth century it is today *Tarsus*, vilayet of Içel, S Turkey in Asia. From 550 A.D. sericulture and the silk industry flourished in the towns of Asia Minor (see *EB* XX, 664–65, *s.v.* "Silk and Sericulture") and it is *a priori* more likely that Tarsus should have been identified with this product than *Tartarye* I (despite the *NED s.v.* "tars"; Skeat V, 85; Manly 555).

The word, whatever its origin, appears in OFr as *tarse*, whence Chaucer's form.

Tartarye [land of] [var. MR VI, 508], Tatary, less correctly but often Tartary (the first, false *r* presumably somehow under the influence of Classical *Tartarus*), land of the Tatars (see *Tatre*), is a loose geographical term, at one time or another including any or all areas from the Black Sea or Volga, eastward through north-central Asia, to the Manchurian coast of the Yellow Sea. Chaucer clearly uses the name with two quite distinct applications:

I. In *BD* 1025, where it is closely associated with *Carre Nar* and *Drye See, Tartarye* may be supposed to refer to the old Tartar homeland in Outer Mongolia (cp. G & I *passim*) and is mentioned as a region to which the Duchess of Lancaster would not have sent an admirer on an irksome or futile mission (cp. *Alysaundre, Carre Nar, Drye See, Pruyce, Turkye, Walakye*).

II. In *CT* F 9 the *land of Tartarye* (in F 71 *this lond*) in which *Sarray* is said to be located, refers to the steppes of southern Russia or Polovtsian steppes, an area without exact boundaries but corresponding roughly to the Tatar Autonomous Soviet Socialist Republic, also Tatarstan; during most of Chaucer's life-time it was under the weakening rule of the Western Kypchaks (G & I 21 ff.). On this western Mongol empire, the Golden Horde, founded by Batu Khan, see G & I 63 ff.

Tatre [var. MR VI, 510, 531], (1) sb., a Tatar, inhabitant of *Tartarye* II, is used in *CT* F 28 to identify one Cambyus Kan (not answering formally to Chinggis Khan); (2) adj., in F 266 likewise identifying Cambyus Kan.

The native name *Tatar*, of unknown etymology, referred originally to a small ethnic group defeated by the Mongols (cp. G & I 43 ff.), yet whose name came to be extended by neighboring peoples to include the Mongols and hence is virtually identical with the latter.

Tessalie, see **T(h)essalie,** below.

Tewnes [var. *Twnes* for *Tuunes*], Tunis, capital city of the republic of Tunisia, formerly a French protectorate (*Tunisie*), on the Lake of Tunis or the Bahira which communicates with the Mediterranean, replaced Carthage (*Cartage, MS* V, 113) in importance and in Moslem times became the chief city of the area. It is mentioned in *BD* 310 in a punning rhyme with *entunes* (var. *entewnes*) "songs" as a *toun* for which Chaucer would not exchange the pleasure of the bird-calls to which he is listening.

The name looks back to Lat. *Tūnēs, -ētis*, OFr *Tunes*, whence Chaucer's form.

Theban, adj. [Lat. *Thēbanus*], pertaining to *1 Thebes* (below), Theban, usually with reference to the two noble kinsmen, Palamon and/or Arcite: *Anel* 85, 210, *TC* 5, 601, *CT* A 2515, 2526, F 1432, 1434.

Sb., inhabitant of *1 Thebes*: *Anel* 60, *CT* A 1877, 2570, 2623, 2829, 2882, 2974.

Chaucer's form is directly adapted from Latin.

I. **Thebes** [Lat. *Thēbae*], chief city of the ancient Greek state of Boeotia, situated *ca* 35 m. NE of *Athenes* (above), is in Chau-

cer essentially thought of as in the time of the legendary King
Creon and the wars of the "Seven". It is mentioned often in
connection with some person or event of the wars of the Seven
and especially frequently in the Knight's Tale: *TC* 5, 937, 1486,
1490; *LGW* F 421 (G409); *CT* A 933, 967, 983, 986, 1002, 1203,
1283, 1331, 1355, 1383, 1483, 1548, 1793, 1880, 2658, D 741,
746, E 1716, 1721, H 116. In *CT* A 939, 1544, B·289 it is *T.
the cité*; *Anel* 66, *TC* 5, 1486, *CT* A 989, 1549, E 1721, H 117
it is a *cité*, and a *toun* in *Anel* 68, 70, 72, *TC* 5, 1510, *CT* A 936,
1548. Its ramparts (*wall, walles*) are mentioned in *CT* A 990,
1331 (*waste*), 1880 (*wyde*), and the same, i.e., the "seven-gated"
wall of the legendary king Amphion, is mentioned in *CT* H
117 (*walled the cité*). There is a temple of Mars (*Anel* 355–56).
Outside the town is a *feeld* or open country (*CT* A 984, 1003).

   In *Anel* 53 *Thebes*, presumably standing for Boeotia, is contrasted to the rest of Greece; Boeotia is also implied in *contré*
of *CT* A 1004, 1383. In *TC* 5, 602, *hem of Thebes* stands for
Thebans sb. above().

   The war of the "Seven" is specifically referred to in *TC* 2,
107 (*assege*), *CT* A 937 (*seege*), B 200 (*strif*); the town is said
to have been burned (*TC* 5, 1510) and afterward was *desolat*
and *bare* (*Anel* 62). Statius' *Thebaid*, dealing with this subject,
is alluded to in *HF* 1460 (3, 370), *Anel* 10 (*storie in Latyn*;
cp. l. 21); *TC* 2, 83–84 (*geste of the seege of Thebes*, and cp. 2,
108), 100 (*romaunce*), and though wrongly, in *CT* A 2294
("*Stace of Thebes*") where the source is in fact Boccaccio's
Teseida.

   The *broche of Thebes*, described at length in *Mars* 245–62,
actually refers to a bracelet made by Vulcan-Haephestus to
bring misfortune on Harmonia, daughter of Mars and Venus,
and subsequent owners. The story is told in Statius' *Thebaid*

II, 265 ff. It was worn inauspiciously by Argia on the occasion of her marriage to Polynices of Thebes.

Chaucer's form is OFr *T(h)ebes* (mod. *Thebes*), in turn based on Lat. acc. pl. *Thēbās*.

II. Thebes [Lat. *Thēbae*], Greek name of the ancient Egyptian city of *Wesi*, later Ne "the city", on the Nile some 400 m. above its mouth, was the ancient capital of Upper Egypt on whose site Karnak and Luxor now stand. The Greeks seem to have applied the name of *1 Thebes* to the Egyptian site because of some fancied resemblance, perhaps the numerous gates common to both. It is mentioned in *CT* A 1472 to define *nercotikes and opie ... fyn*, on whose traditional association with the Egyptian city, see O. F. Emerson, "Chaucer's 'Opie of Thebes Fyn'", *Modern Philology* XVII (1919–20), 287–91.

T[h]essalie, Thessaly [Lat. *Thessalia*], NE division of Greece south of Macedonia (*Macedoine*, above), with Larissa its chief city, is mentioned as the kingdom of Pelleus and home of Jason in *LGW* 1396, 1461, 1533, 1619, 1654; in *LGW* 1651 it is referred to as *hom*. It is Pelleus' *regne* (*LGW* 1401), a *lond* (1403), a *regioun* (1412), a *contré* (1461) and in *CT* B *3869 (2679) the scene of Julius Caesar's attack on Pompey.

Chaucer's form is OFr.

Tholosan [Lat. *Tolosanus*], adj., of or pertaining to Toulouse (Lat. *Tolosa*), dept. Haute-Garonne, France, in antiquity a city in Gallia Narbonensis. In *HF* 1460 (3, 370) it is applied wrongly to the Neapolitan poet Publius Papinus Statius (45–96 A.D.), an error Chaucer may have picked up from Dante.

Chaucer's form with ornamental, silent *h*, is adapted from Latin; cp. *Mantoan*, above.

Tybre, the central Italian river Tiber [Lat. *Tiberis*, Ital. *Tevere*] which rises in the Tuscan Apennines, cuts through Rome, crosses the Roman Campagna, and enters the Mediterranean (Tyrrhenian) Sea at Ostia. It is mentioned in *CT* B *3666 (2476) as a river in which the Emperor Nero liked to fish with nets of thread of gold.

Chaucer's form is the semi-learned OFr (and mod. Fr.) *Tibre* vs popular OFr *Teivre, Toivre*, forms found also in ME.

Tigrys, the Tigris [Lat. *Tigris*], with the Euphrates the lesser of two great rivers of ancient Mesopotamia, today answering essentially to Iraq, is in *Bo* 5, m. 1, ll. 1–2 (1640–45) wrongly said to rise from a common source with the Euphrates (*Eufrates*, above). The Tigris is the Hiddekel of *Gen.* ii, 14, *Dan.* x, 4.

Chaucer's form is Latin.

Tyle, [Ultima] Thule [Lat. *Thyle, Tyle*, rarely *Thule*], from the time (330 B.C.) of Pytheas of Massilia (Marseilles) was thought of as an island in the extreme north of Europe; it has been a matter of almost endless conjecture whether Pytheas meant Iceland (otherwise unknown until the ninth century A.D.) or some other island between Iceland and Britain. The name Thule, reminiscent of *Ultima Thule* of antiquity, was given to the site of the present weather-station and airbase up the north-west coast of Greenland in 1910 by Peter Freuchen, who with his friend Knud Rasmussen, started the first settlement for white men there; see his *Vagrant Viking: My Life and Adventures* (New York, 1953), esp. pp. 7, 90, and Index p. 421, *s.v.* It is mentioned in *Bo* 3, m. 5, l. 8 (740–45) as one terminus of a long distance; in l. 7 it is *the laste ile in the See* (i.e., *Occian*, above).

Chaucer's form answers to the Lat. type *T(h)yle*, preferred until the time of the Renaissance.

Tyrene, adj. Tyrrhenian, Etruscan, Etrurian [Lat. *Tyrrhenius*], referring to that part of the Mediterranean lying between the Italian mainland and the islands of Corsica, Sardinia and Sicily, is used in *Bo* 3, m. 8, l. 10 (795–800) to define the Tiber (*watir that highte Tyrene*) as a river flowing into the Tyrrhenian Sea (cp. *flumen Tyrrhenium, Aen.* 7, 663). This *watir* (*NED s.v.* 12c) has *foordes* convenient for huntsmen. Then are dealt with certain fine things to be got from the *see* (pearls, tender fish, sea-urchins) which presumably is the Tyrrhenian Sea proper (cp. *Tyrrhena vada, Aen.* 1, 67).

Tyrie, Tyre, an important town of ancient Phoenicia [Lat. *Tyrus, -i*, f.], now the unimportant town of Çur under the government of Beirut, is mentioned in *Bo* 2, m. 5, ll. 12, 15 (475–80) in connection with the famous purple crimson dye (*venym of Tyrie*) extracted from the bodies of certain molluscs (*a maner schelle-fyssch*) used to dye cloth (*purpre*) or wool; similarly in *Bo* 3, m. 4, l. 3 (715–20) there is mention of *faire purpres of Tyrie* for purple cloth, the dress of emperors or kings (see *NED* "purple" B. 1a and "purper" B I).

Chaucer's form through OFr represents an adaptation of the Lat. adj. *Tyrius* "of, pertaining to Tyre" in Boethius (*Tyrio ... veneno*).

Tyro, a Tyrian, man of Tyre [Lat. *Tyrus, -i* f. Tyre], is used in *CT* B 81 in the combination *Tyro Appollonius* to refer to the novelist Apollonius of Tyre (Lat. *Apollonius de Tyro*) of uncertain date and identity, where Chaucer has evidently taken the abl. *Tyro* as the nom. of a sb. *Tyro, -onis* (cp. *Macedo*, above).

Tolletanes [var. MR VI, 634], OFr plur. adj., of or pertaining to Toledo, Spain, Toledan, is used probably not quite accurately in *CT* F 1273 to describe a set of astronomical tables used by a scholar of *Orliens* (cp. F 1274–79). Formally Chaucer's *Tables Tolletanes* "Tables of Toledo" should refer to a set of astronomical tables first edited by Azaraquil in the eleventh century but subsequently rendered obsolete by the so-called *Alfonsine Tables*, drawn up by Jean de Linières *ca* 1320. It is unlikely that Chaucer or anyone else in his day would have any use for, or interest in, the older set; yet the old term lingered on and was, as surely here, applied wrongly to the later and more up-to-date tables. On all this see Derek J. Price, *The Equatorie of the Planetis* (Cambridge University Press, 1955), esp. pp. 79–80, with ample literature.

The French title *Tables tolletanes*, rendering Lat. *Tabulae Toletanae*, is here taken over bodily; the Lat. adj. is based on Roman (Iberian?) *Tolētum*, ancient capital of the Iberian tribe of the *Carpetāni* (Holder I, 807–08), later of the Visigoths, later still of the old kingdom of Castile.

Trace, Thrace [Lat. *Thracia, Threcia*], in antiquity an area in northern Greece, in the course of history of fluctuating boundaries and centering on the mountain range of Rhodope (*Rodopeya,-peye*, above) and the river Hebrus, rising in Mt Haemus and flowing into the Thracian Sea, mod. Maritza(?) was in Chaucer's time under Turkish sway.

It is mentioned as being reached from Athens by rowing in *LGW* 2308–09 (cp. l. 2361, *from Atthenes in a barge*). It is the homeland of Phyllis, daughter of King Sithon of Thrace (*HF* 391), also is a *lond* (*LGW* 2423, 2427, 2434), reached by Demophon from Troy be sea (*se*: ll. 2405, 2419). In *Bo* 3, m. 12, l.

4 (1115–20) it is the home of Orpheus (*poete of Trace*), and in *LGW* 2244 Tereus, kinsman of Mars and husband of Procne, is lord of the land. The worship of Mars and the *grete temple* are alluded to in *Anel* 1–4 (*Trace*, l. 2) and in *CT* A 1972. Among the supporters of Palamon is Lycurgus, *the grete king of Trace* (*CT* A 2129), legendary king of the Thracian tribe of the Edones (cp. Statius' *Thebaid* IV, 386; VII, 180); the latter's garb and his fondness for hunting lion and deer (*CT* A 2137–50) are in keeping with other descriptions of the region (*contré*, A 2137). The wildness of the country and its unfriendly climate are emphasized in *Anel* 2 (*frosty contré*), *CT* A 1973 (*colde, frosty regioun*), while the forbidding countryside is pictured in murals in the oratory of Mars (*CT* A 1975–94). In the Legend of Philomela (*LGW* 2310–12, 2362) something is made of a forest and dark cave, and in *CT* A 1639–42 Thrace is a land where the lion and the bear are hunted.

In two situations Thrace has untraditionally been confused with or substituted for Thessaly (*Tessalie*, above): in *HF* 1572 (3, 482), 1585 (3, 495, *a contré*), 1789 (3, 699) it is the home of Aeolus, god of the winds, who lives and rules there as king; traditionally Aeolus' home was in the Lipari islands, between Italy and Sicily; here there is confusion with Aeolus, a king in Thessaly and grandson of Deucalion (cp. Servius on Virgil, *Aen.* 6, 585). Again in *LGW* F 432 (G 422) Alcestis is spoken of as *whilom quene of Trace*, whereas her husband Admetus was king of Pelasgis, a district of Thessaly (Thessalia Pelasgiotis) with his residence in Pherae, now Velestino.

Chaucer's form is OFr.

Tramissene [var. MR V, 6], Tlemcen or Tlemsen, dép. Oran, NW Algeria (French since 1842, today of disputed status), was in Chaucer's day a great center of trade and chief city of the Berber dynasty of the Beni or Banu Marin (*Bel-Marye*) or the Marinide dynasty in the Arab *al-Maghrib al-Aqsa* ("The Far West"), an area approximating western Algeria and Morocco (*Marrok*); see *E Isl* IV, 801–08. It is mentioned in *CT* A 62 as a place where the Knight had fought (cp. *Algezir, Bel-Marye, Gernade*).

The name looks back to Berber *tilma* "spring, well", plur. *tilimsān*, and means "(town of) springs or wells". Forms with a western substitution of *r* for *l* appear in Froissart: *Tramessemes, Tremessemes*, later *Tremesen, Tremecen* (Cook 233, and n. 7, Skeat V, 7, nn. 56–58), and on such, no doubt OFr forms Chaucer's form depends. Modern Tlemcen is adapted directly from Berber-Arabic.

Troian, Troyen, adj. and sb. [Lat. *Troiānus*].

A. adj. pertaining to Troy or its inhabitants, is used of a song (*TC* 2, 825), of the Trojan legend (*gestes, TC* 1, 145), of the Trojans Aeneas (*HF* 217), Calkas (*TC* 4, 71–72, 332), Ripheus (*TC* 4, 53), and of the Trojan nation (*HF* 207).

B. sb., sg. and pl., an inhabitant or native of Troy, occurs in *HF* 156, *TC* 2, 977 (var. *Troyens*), 4, 107, 1490, 5, 122, 126, 141, 877, 912, 920; *LGW* 933, and is used specifically of Aeneas in *LGW* 1172, 1211, 1265. For circumlocutions to express "Trojan, sb." see *Troie*, below (*folk of, they, hem of T.*).

Chaucer's form *Troian* looks back to Lat. *Troiānus* perhaps by way of Ital. *Troiano* (cp. *Mantoan, Tholsan*, above), while *Troien* is OFr, in turn from Lat. *Troiānus*.

Troianyssh, adj. Trojan and equivalent to *Troian* A, above, is used in *HF* 201 to define "blood", i.e., "lineage, race". It is

formed from *Troian*, above, with the OE suffix *-isc*, ME *-ish*.
Cp. *Grekyssh*, above.

Troie, Troy [Lat. *Troia*, Turk. *Truva*], of which Ilium, the
old poetical name, is the ancient fortified Thraco-Phrygian
town (Troy VII, 2 of the archaeologists), whose site is commonly
identified with the mound of Hisarlik (Turk. "place of fortress"),
Biga, villayet of Canakkale (= Dardanelles, ancient Hellespont), Turkey. Hisarlik lies some 3–4 m. in from the west end
of the Dardanelles and in the fork above the juncture of the
Dümberek su (*Symois*, above) and the Mendere çayı (Maeander
or Pinarbasi çayı (Scamander), the latter flowing into the Dardanelles east of the promontory of Yenesehir (Lat. *Sigeum*).
Essentially because of its prominence in *TC*, *Troie* is by far
the most frequently used geographical name in Chaucer and
the one about which most is told. In *TC* many invented details
are supplied and it is clear that Chaucer pictured Troy as much
like his own London; see *Mediaeval Studies*, VII (1945), 96–97,
133–35, for a similar treatment of Etzeln burc and Worms by
the author of the *Nibelungenlied*.

> "In Troy, there lies the scene,"
> Shakespeare, *TC*, Prol. l. 1.

Troy is often mentioned as the scene of the Graeco-Trojan
war and especially in *TC* as the place in which persons involved
in the war find themselves (*assege, sege, were*); it is the place
from which they come, to which they go, and the like: *CT* A
2833, B 288, *4419 (3229), F 210, 1446, G 975 (size emphasized);
BD 1066, 1120; *Bo* 4, m. 7, ll. 4–5 (1595–1600); *TC* 1, 59 (*to-
Troie-wardes*), 68, 74, 119; 2, 644; 3, 357, 1441, 1452; 4, 77, 91,
93, 119, 140, 336, 533, 661, 1307, 1343, 1441, 1549, 1558, 1630;

5, 28, 45, 91, 197, 393, 426, 609, 616, 729, 765, 779, 874, 912, 916, 960, 1380, 1546, 1662. It is occasionally *Troie town*: *TC* 4, 30; 5, 768, 856, 969, 1006, 1649, also *town of Troie* in *TC* 2, 139, 748, 881; 3, 874; 4, 126, 204–05. In *TC* it is often alluded to merely as *town*: 1, 64, 75, 86, 141, 186, 558, 1076; 2, 189, 378, 379, 737 (*noble town*), 1416; 3, 383, 570, 577, 1772, 1782; 4, 62, 79, 112, 118, 121, 126 (var.), 192, 204, 209, 401, 531, 547, 553, 585, 1340, 1380, 1386; 5, 5, 400, 429, 563, 677, 990, 1154; less usually as a *cité*: *Troies cité* (*TC* 1, 100), *Troye the cité* (*LGW* 2404), or merely *cité* in *TC* 1, 59, 129, 149; 2, 1146; 4, 685, 1205, 1479; 5, 906; *LGW* 937. Thrice it is a *place*: *TC* 5, 245, 710, 956. In *TC* 1, 2, 609; 3, 791, 1715; 4, 276, *Troie* identifies the Trojan royal dynasty, in *CT* F 548 it identifies Paris, in *CT* F 306 the siege, in *BD* 1247–48 and *Bo* 4, m. 7, ll. 4–5 (1595–1600) the destruction of the city, and twice the history of the legend of the city: *BD* 326 and *LGW* 1153–54 (cp. *Troian gestes* under *Troian*, above). *Troye contré* (*HF* 146) and *contré* (*LGW* 938, 1279) is the surrounding district of the Troad, also referred to as the *lond* in *HF* 172, *LGW* 1026. A plural form, *thousand Troyes*, is used in *TC* 2, 977 (cp. *Greces twelve* of *TC* 5, 924). It is implied though wrongly that the *Symois* (above) flows through the town (cp. *se* of *TC* 4, 1548–49). Its size is stressed in *CT* G 975.

Troie is also used in several locutions for the adj. *Troian/ Troien*: so *blood of Troie* "Trojan lineage" (*TC* 5, 600, and cp. *Troianyssche blood* of *HF* 201); *folk of T.* (*TC* 1, 138, 160; 4, 48, 55, 122; 5, 93, 119, 856 [*folk of T. toun*], 883; *LGW* 1151); *they (hem) of Troie* (*TC* 1, 135, 136, 148, 150 [var.]).

The ramparts (*wal, walles*) of Troy are mentioned in *CT* B 288 and in *TC* 4, 121, 1482; 5, 733, 1145; in *TC* 5, 666, 1112, 1194 the town-walls are wide enough to walk along. Town-gates are likewise noted: *TC* 2, 615, and in *TC* 5, 32, 603, 1138, 1140, 1178, 1192 the gate (sg. and pl.) in question is that by which Criseyde leaves the Greek camp. The gate of *TC* 2, 617–18 is that named for Dardanus, legendary ancestor of the Trojan race, whose name survives in the modern name Dardanelles. The town is marked by high towers and conspicuous buildings from which the Greek camp is visible (*TC* 5, 729).

In antiquity the citadel of Troy was *Pergama* (neut. pl.) or *Pergamum* (neut. sg.); among medieval writers this was supplanted by Ilium, Chaucer's *Ilio(u)n*, above, not mentioned in *TC* though elsewhere: *noble tour of Ylioun* (*LGW* 936), also in *HF* 158, *CT* B 289, *4546 (3356); *castel* (*HF* 163) seems to refer to Ilium, also described as the chief donjon (*dongeoun*) of Troy (*LGW* 937). The pairing *of Troie and of Ilyoun* in *BD* 1248 suggests that Chaucer may have thought of Ilium as an enclave, a town within Troy.

Of the lay-out of the interior of the town little is told, but several scattered architectural monuments are featured, though nothing is said of their relative positions. There are many temples (*TC* 3, 383); one in 3, 540–46 is dedicated to Apollo; special emphasis is given to the temple containing the image of Pallas, the Palladium (*Palladion*) of *TC* 1, 162, 185 (*large*), 267, 317, 323, 363; 5, 566, the portal (*dore*) to which is mentioned in *TC* 1, 180. Another temple is mentioned in *BD* 1068, while in *TC* 5, 564–81 various sites (*places*) are mentioned cursorily. A marble statue of Niobe weeping for her children is mentioned in *TC* 1, 699–700 and is alluded to later in *TC* 1, 759. A House of Parliament is clearly assumed, though only the parliamentary assembly is actually mentioned (*TC* 4, 143, 148 [*place*], 211, 217, 218, 344, 558–59, 664, 1297). The wooden horse, introduced into the town by Sinon, is mentioned in *CT* F 209, *HF* 155.

Prominent as the setting of much of the action are the residences of Criseyde, Deiphebus, Pandarus, Sarpedon, and Troilus; these Chaucer must have pictured as resembling the dwellings of the wealthy and the great of fourteenth-century London.

Criseyde's residence is a *paleys* (*paleis*) in *TC* 2, 76, 1094, 1252 (*to paleis ward*); 5, 523, 525, 540, 542, 546; a *hous* in 1, 127; 2, 437, 1461; 3, 1581; 4, 823; 5, 528, 541, 575; a *place* in 2, 1013; 3, 218; 4, 1685; 5, 534; it is apostrophized in 5, 540–53, where it is a shrine (5, 553). It is on a *strete* (2, 1015, 1186, 1248 and implicitly so in 3, 1782) with a house across the street (2, 1188, 1189), and is apparently thought of as somewhat outside, or on the outskirts of the town (cp. 2, 1146; *the cité which that stondeth yondre*). At the back of her house is a large *gardyn* (2, 814, 819, 1114, 1117), also called a *yerd* "yard" (2, 820); this garden is laid out with shaded and sanded walks (*aleyes*) along which are newly placed benches (2, 820, 822) and is reached from the palace by a set of steps (*steyre*, 2, 813 and implied in 2, 1117), leading down from the ground floor room (*chaumbre*, 2, 1117). Downstairs is also a *halle* for dining and assembly (2, 1170 ff.; 4, 732), also a *parlour* or living-room (2, 82) presumably smaller than the great hall, with a floor paved with flags, tiles or mosaic (*paved*, 2, 82). Upstairs is a small room or boudoir (*closet*, 2, 599, 1215), Criseyde's bedroom (*chaumbre*, 4, 732–33, 1701, and perhaps 2, 1173), and a living-room with some sort of bay-window (2, 1186, 1192, and cp. 2, 1015), evidently handsomely furnished (2, 1228–29 and cp. 4, 1380). In 5, 531, 534 the place has been closed up and the doors and windows boarded.

Deiphebus' residence is a *hous* (2, 1514, 1540); its existence is implied in 2, 1364 (*a certeyn place*), 1402, 1438, 1480. Like Criseyde's it has a garden (*herber greene*, 2, 1705; *gardyn*, 3, 221) connected with the building by steps (*steire*: 2, 1705; 3, 205, implied in 3, 191). The *grete chaumbre* (2, 1712) would be the great hall, off which is a small room (*chaumbre*: 2, 1646, implied in 2, 1725 [*inward*]).

Pandarus' residence is a *hous* (3, 195, 560, 635). A dining-room is implied in 3, 607; on the same floor with this appear to be sleeping quarters (cp. *yonder*: 3, 663). This is all on the ground floor, if one accepts the existence of the drain (*goter*: 3, 787) between the house and outside mentioned by Pandarus; that Troilus did not enter through it is immaterial. Two attempts have been made to work out a ground-plan with particular thought as to the bedroom arrangements. I attempted this in *MS* XV (1953), 134–35 (omitted here), where on p. 135 the door between Troilus' room and Criseyde's should be marked '*e*', the one between Criseyde's and the corridor '*f*'. Better as being simpler and less specific is the discussion by H. M. Smyser, 'The Domestic Background of *Troilus and Criseyde*', *Speculum*, XXXI (1956), 297–315, floor-plan, p. 298. It may well be questioned whether Chaucer ever had a precisely worked out blue-print in mind.

Sarpedon's country-place is said to be a mile from Troilus' palace (5, 403); there Troilus and Pandarus spend a week (5, 434–500).

Troilus' residence is a *paleys* in 1, 324; 2, 933, 1537; 3, 1529, 1534 (*real p.*); 5, 201, 512–13. In 5, 527 it seems to be viewed as a little out of town, as is Criseyde's palace, above. It has a *gardyn* (2, 508; 3, 1738) with a spring (*welle*: 2, 508) presumably forming a pool. Of the interior one hears chiefly of Troilus' bedroom (*chaumbre*: 1, 358, 547; 2, 556, 935; 4, 220, 354; 5, 202, 292) with door, window, and walls metioned in 4, 232–33, 244, 352; here Troilus spends a good fair bit of his time and commonly in bed. In 5, 514 *chaumbre* refers to a dining-room (cp. 5, 518).

Priam's court, unimportant in the action of the poem, is mentioned in 4, 1392–93.

Little is told of the environs of Troy. Out toward the Greek camp which is visible from Troy (cp. 5, 730) runs a long *valeye* (5, 67, actually mistranslating Boccaccio's *vallo* "rampart"). Some of the surrounding country is thought of as wooded (5, 1144) and accessible from the besieged town (4, 1521 ff.) despite Diomedes' statement that the Trojans *in prisoun ben* (5, 883–84). Somewhere between Troy and the Greek camp is a *feld* or piece of open country (1, 1074; 2, 195) where fighting goes on except in time of truce.

The war and the siege, forming a somewhat dominating backdrop to the poem is referred to as *assege* (1, 464; 2, 107); *assegeden* (1, 60); *sege* (2, 123; 4, 1480), and as *werre* (2, 868(?); 3, 1772; 4, 547; 5, 855). In *CT* F 306 it is the *grete sege of Troie*.

Chaucer's form of the name is OFr.

Trumpington, Trumpington [C], a village 2 m. S of Cambridge out Trumpington St, is mentioned in *CT* A 3921 [var. *Thorpynton*, MR V, 389] as near the site of a *mille* (A 3923, 4008, 4021, 4061, 4115, 4242, 4311); in A 3943, 3977, 4135 it is a *toun*. The mill site is the spot "Old Mills" on the Ordnance Survey map and was obviously on the original channel of the Grante or Cam over which went a bridge (A 3922), called a *brook* (A 3922, 3923, Bourne Brook) in the surrounding *fen* (A 4065, 4080, 4091). Skeat V, 116 seems to think that Chaucer could not have known Cambridge or known it well, otherwise he would not have made the boys feel that they had to spend the night out at the mill (A 4177); this may all be quite true, but in view of the state of medieval roads the boys may very well have felt that to ride back in the dark might have resulted in the horse breaking a leg or themselves breaking their necks. See Manly 561; *PN* XIX *C* 2; Muirhead *England* 580.

The name looks back to OE *Trumpinga-tún* "village of *Trumpa's people", based on an unrecorded personal name *Trumpa*, perhaps "surly fellow".

Turkye, Turkey [Fr. *Turquie*, Turk. *Türkiye*] in Chaucer's day comprised essentially the present-day Turkey-in-Asia, an area then mostly ruled by Ottoman and Seljuk Turks. It is mentioned in *BD* 1026 as a land to which the Duchess of Lancaster would not have sent an admirer on an irksome or futile mission (cp. *Alysaundre, Carre Nar, Drye See, Pruyce, Tartarye* I, *Walakye*). In *CT* A 66 it is a pagan (Moslem) country where the Knight had fought (cp. the Turkish towns of *Lyeys, Palatye, Satalye*).

Chaucer's form is French, based on Med. Lat. *Turchia* or *Turquia*, a regional name based on OFr *Turc*, Med. Lat. *Turcus* "Turk" of unknown origin; see *NED s.v.* "Turk".

Turkeys [var. MR V, 283], Turkish, of or pertaining to the Turks, is used in *CT* A 2895 to describe a shooting bow with a golden case (unless referring to a quiver for the arrows [*arwes in the caas*] as in *CT* A 2358) and fittings. The Turkish bow owed its excellence to its composite character of horn, wood, and sinew, in that order from front to back (vs bows just of yew).

Chaucer's form is OFr *turkeis*, Fr. *turquois* (fem. *turquoise* yielding the name of the gem-stone), based on *Turkye*; English "Turkish" is a late formation with the English suffix *-ish*.

V

valence in *PF* 272 is the name of some sheer (*subtyl*) fabric used for kerchiefs and is presumably based on the name of the town of Valence on the Rhone (dép. Drôme), France. For the name of other materials based on place names or defined by them see *chalon*, *Reynes*, and *Tars*.

The Latin town-name *Valentia*, based on the gentile name *Valentius*, here represented is exceedingly common and is, for instance, identical with Valencia in E Spain; the present town is mentioned by Pliny and was also known in antiquity as *Julia Valentia* and *Valentia Segovellaunorum*, also shortened to *Segalaunorum* (Holder II, 1451–52); see Gröhler I, 297–98.

Venyse, Venice [Ital. *Venezia*, Fr. *Venise*, Germ. *Venedig*], Italy, is mentioned in *HF* 1348 (3, 258) to describe a ducat of very pure gold content; on Venetian gold ducats see *NED s.v.* "ducat", 1 and 1b. In *CT* E 51 *Venyse*, as *Venetia* in Petrarch (B & D 296, 8), is mentioned to indicate the point where the *Poo* empties through several mouths into the Adriatic; but by *Venetia* Petrarch (from whom Chaucer derives his statement) can only have been thinking in a most general way of the ancient territory of the *Veneti* (cp. his *Flaminia* under *Ferrare*, above), perhaps that portion of the Lombard plain known as the Veneto, since he surely knew that none of the mouths of the Po flowed into the sea nearer than 35–40 m. S of the city of Venice. Whether Chaucer in imitating Petrarch knew this can scarcely be determined and is of trifling consequence.

The name of the town and region is based on the tribal (Venetic) name *Veneti*; Holder III, 160–67; Matthias 302–07. Chaucer's and the modern English form are French.

Verone, Verona [Lat. *Verona*] on the Adige (Germ. *Etsch*), prov. of Verona, in antiquity in Gallia Transpadana, is in *Bo* 1, pr. 4, l. 235 (155–60) a *cité* where Boethius legally defended one Albyn (l. 239), probably Decius Albinus.

Chaucer's form is OFr; on this name see further *MS*, VII (1945), 91–92, under "*Berne*".

[Mount] Vesulus [Lat.] [var. MR VI, 248, 249], Monte Viso or more commonly Monviso, NE Italy, highest peak (12,615 ft) of the Cottian Alps, first conquered in 1861; this mountaineering achievement inspired the formation in the following year of the famous Club Alpino Italiano. Monviso, near the French frontier and about 42 m. SW of Turin, is mentioned in *CT* E 58 as having at its base (*roote*) the source of the *Poo*; it is also mentioned in E 47.

The name looks back to Rom. (*Mons*) *Vesulus*; Holder III, 261; *EI* XXXV, 455–56.

Visevus, Vesuvius [Lat. *Vesuvius, Vesevus, Vesaevus*], celebrated volcano in the ancient province of Campania (*Campayne*, above), rising from the eastern border of the Bay of Naples, is in *Bo* 1, m. 4, ll. 8–10 (90–95) called an *unstable mountaigne* with reference to its eruptions; Boethius probably knew directly of those of 472 and 512 A.D. The further description in ll. 10–11: *that writhith out thruw his brokene chemeneyes* (= lateral vents or fumaroles) *smokynge fires* (= characteristic emission of vapor) is accurate.

Chaucer's *Visevus* looks back to the collateral Lat. *Vesevus*, here used by Boethius.

W

Walakye, Walachia or Wallachia [Med. Lat. *Walachia,* Fr. *Valachie*], an area between the Danube and the Transylvanian

Alps in S Romania and since 1859 a part of Romania, was in Chaucer's day an independent Romanic-speaking kingdom which under Vladislav Bassarab (1364–74) accepted Hungarian over-lordship. It is mentioned in *BD* 1024 as a region to which the Duchess of Lancaster would not have sent an admirer on an irksome or futile mission (cp. *Alysaundre, Carre Nar, Drye See, Pruyce, Tartarye* I, *Turkye*).

The name looks back to a Celtic base *Volc-* (cp. Caesar's *Volcae*), yielding Germanic *Walh-* (see *Wales*, below), first applied to Celts, including Britons, later to Romanic-speaking peoples of southern Europe. See *NED* under "Vlach", "walach", "Welsh", also *MS* VII, 129–30 under "Walache".

Wales, the principality of Wales, is mentioned in *CT* B 544 as a refuge of pre-Saxon, Late British Christians who had fled from Deira (i.e., *Northumberlond*) before the days of King Ælla.

The name looks back to OE *Wéalas* (sing. *Wealh*) "Britons"; cp. *Walakye*, above.

Ware, a place-name Ware, is mentioned in *CT* A 692 to define one limit of the Pardoner's territory or beat (see *Berwyck*, above) and in A 4336 as the home town of Roger the Cook. There are three Wares of any consequence in England: most pominent is Ware on the Lea (Herts; *PN* XV *Herts* 206–07), in the fourteenth century the site of a Franciscan monastery, the limit of John Gilpin's ride, and whose vicar Charles Chauncy became the second president of Harvard University (1654–72). There are also two hamlets of this name, one near Sandwich (K) and one (Ware Cross or Barton) by Kingsteignton (D). The name is also applied to numerous private places which cannot enter into the question here. It is probably impossible, as in the case of *Berwyck*, to determine definitely which Ware Chaucer had in mind; in the case of Roger the Cook it would be of no consequence (Manly 53, Bowden 187 assume the Herts Ware). In the case of the Pardoner, where *Ware* is opposed to *Berwyck* and is thus intended to indicate the geographical extent of the latter's fund-raising activities, it would be of some little point to know. The Herts Ware is probably the best bet.

The name almost certainly looks back to OE *wer* m. or the byform *wær* "weir, fishing pool"; *DEPN s.v.*; *PN* XV *Herts* 206–07.

Wateryng of Seint Thomas, a lost site, St Thomas Watering, S.E.1 (Sr), close to the second mile-stone on the Old Kent Road (see *Caunterbury Wey*) is mentioned in *CT* A 826 as a spring or road-brook where the pilgrims halted and presumably watered their horses (cp. *NED* "watering" sb., 15b). The site is mentioned from Chaucer to Ben Jonson (1630), after which it drops out of use. See Littlehales 10; *PN* XI *Sr* 5 *ad fin.*

The significance of the name seems to be "watering place for horses or cattle on the road to the shrine of, or dedicated to, St Thomas à Becket", martyred (A.D. 1170) archbishop of Canterbury; *PN* XI *Su* 5.

Watlynge-Strete, Watling-Street, said in *HF* 939 (2, 431) to be what some people call the "*Galaxie*" *HF* 936 [2, 428]) or "*Milky Wey*" (*HF* 937 [2, 429]); on this extension of the old Roman highway-name see *NED s.v.*, 2, for instances from Chaucer to 1590; now obsolete. See Muirhead *England* 17.

OE *Wæclinga stræt* is the old native name for the Roman road running from near London through St Albans (Herts)

(OE *Wæclinga ćeaster*) to Wroxeter (Sa) and Chester, and from the twelfth century on also applied to the road running SE from London to Canterbury and on to Dover (see *Caunterbury Wey*; *NED s.v.* introductory note and 1; *PN* XV *Herts* 7, 86–87).

[**by**] **Weste,** in the west country, the term "west" then as now defining England more or less W of Dorset and S of Bristol, is mentioned in *CT* A 388 to indicate the general region from which the Shipman came, specifically *Dertemouthe*. See *NED* west *adv.* 3a.

[**Westminster, City of, Mx**] even in Chaucer's day was separated from the City proper (see *Londoun*, above) probably by a bar or chain opposite the SE corner of the Law Courts (see *Temple* under *Londoun*). Westminster is not named but is more or less implied in the phrase *of Rouncivale* (*CT* A 670) used to define the Pardoner. *Rouncival*, short for the Hospital and Chapel of St Mary of Rounceval, Augustinian house to which the Pardoner belonged, stood at Charing, later Charing Cross (S.W.1), just E of the ancient royal palace of Whitehall (*PN* XVIII *Mx* 167). "Rouncival" was the English branch of Nuestra Señora de Roncevalles (OFr *Rencevaux*, Fr. *Roncevaux*), prov. of Navarre, Spain, founded in 1229. See Manly 536; Robinson 667, n. 670; Bowden 284–86. The first element of *Ronce-valles* probably looks back to Lat. *rumex* (Fr. *ronce*) "bramble", the name meaning "bramble grown valley".

No direct mention is made of the English Parliament or of Westminster Hall (Muirhead xlv, 90) but it is hard not to think that Chaucer would have had this in mind when he had Theseus tell Emelye that on the advice of "*my parlement*" she is to take Palamon as her husband (*CT* A 3076–81), and even more so, with hinting allusions to Jack Straw, in the case of the Trojan Parliament which decides on the exchange of Criseyde for Antenor (*TC* 4, 143, 211, 217, 218, 344, 377, 559, 1297).

Windesore, Windsor (Berks), on the Thames *ca* 21 m. W of London, is mentioned in *RR* 1250 to define a "lord's son" who may have been a "*bachelere*" dancing with Franchise; similarly in Guillaume de Lorris' *Roman de la Rose* 1228: *Fiz au seignor de Guindesores* (ed. Ernest Langlois, II [Paris, 1920], 63, 305 "notes"), where *Guindesores* is likewise regularly identified with Windsor in Berkshire. The only real question at issue is whom Guillaume and Chaucer may have had in mind in speaking of the "lord's son". As for Guillaume, it is most likely that he thought of the *seignor* as King Arthur who both in Chrétien de Troyes' *Cligès* (cp. ll. 1197–2056 on Arthur's long but successful siege of Windsor Castle) and in the Old-French romance of *Rigomer* appears as the "king of Windsor". In Guillaume the son was probably nobody in particular, his genealogy being merely created to provide him with a background of social elegance. In translating Guillaume Chaucer perhaps or even probably—since he seems to have had little interest in Arthurian romance—knew nothing of these Arthurian associations and is unlikely to have made any personal identification of either the lord or his son. That he, still less Guillaume, was thinking of Henry II and his son Prince Edward, later Edward I (as suggested by Skeat I, 427, n.), strikes me as an improbable and unnecessary consideration.

The etymology of the name is uncertain, though the second element -*ore* very likely looks back to OE *óra* m. "river-bank", here perhaps in the sense of a place suitable for landing. See further *DEPN*, *s.v.*

Y

Yorkshire, the county of Yorkshire, more specifically the East Riding, mentioned in *CT* D 1709 [var. *Engelond*, MR VI, 177] as the county in which the district of *Holdernesse* (*q.v.*) is situated. In Yorkshire beside *Holdernesse* are *Hulle*, [*Knaresborough*], *Sheffeld*.

The county-name is based on the name York, looking back more or less directly to ON *Jǫfurvík*, adapted from OE *Eoforwíc*, in turn adapted from Romano-British *Eburacum*, perhaps a *fundus*-name based on Brit. *eburos* "yew tree"; see *PN* XIV *YER* 278–80.